# Understanding

# IRAs and SEPs

Dearborn
R&R Newkirk
a division of Dearborn Financial Publishing, Inc.

This publication is designed to provide accurate and authoritative information in regard to the subject matter covered. It is sold with the understanding that the publisher is not engaged in rendering legal, accounting or other professional service. If legal advice or other expert assistance is required, the services of a competent professional person should be sought.

©1996 by Dearborn Financial Publishing, Inc.

Published by Dearborn•R&R Newkirk,
a division of Dearborn Financial Publishing, Inc.

Printed in the United States of America.

First Printing, March 1996

ISBN 0-7931-1484-5

Library of Congress Cataloging-in-Publication Data

Understanding IRAs and SEPs.
        p.  cm.
    ISBN 0-7931-1484-5
    1. Individual retirement accounts—United States. 2. Rollovers
(Finance)—United States.
    HG1660.U5I72   1995                          95-20706
    332.024'01—dc20                              CIP

# ••••• Table of Contents

# Acknowledgments

The publisher wishes to acknowledge and thank Carla Gordon, CFP, as the author of this text. Ms. Gordon is a financial planner and instructor in various areas of financial planning for insurance and financial services professionals.

Ms. Gordon is the principal writer of *Principles of Retirement Planning*, which is published by Dearborn Financial Publishing, Inc.

We also wish to thank Jack Trapp, Jr., CLU, ChFC, a specialist in qualified plans, for his perceptive comments and suggestions on tax issues that affect retirement planning.

# ▪▪▪▪▪ Introduction

**M**any people realize that the retirement income provided through Social Security or employer-sponsored retirement plans is simply not enough for them to maintain a comfortable standard of living after retirement. The solution to this "income gap" is the individual retirement account (IRA), which encourages individuals to save for their own retirement by allowing for tax-deferred accumulation of retirement funds and in some cases, tax deductibility of contributions made to the account.

Since their introduction in 1974, IRAs, along with simplified employee pensions (SEPs), have become one of the most popular ways for American workers to save for their retirement. Yet, there are still many potential prospects who don't understand how an IRA works or an IRA's tax-deferred advantages.

This course is designed for insurance producers and financial representatives who want a better understanding of IRAs, SEPs and rollovers, especially when it comes to the rules and regulations that govern these products. Much confusion exists as to who can establish an IRA, the amount that can be contributed each year and exactly how much of that contribution is deductible. The purpose of this course is to clarify some of these complicated issues.

Once you understand how IRAs, SEPs and rollovers function, you'll be better prepared to help your clients meet their own retirement objectives. This material will give you the necessary knowledge to explain to your clients and prospects the advantages of many retirement-related investment opportunities.

Rick Paszkiet
Editor

# 1

# Introduction to IRAs

Individual retirement accounts (IRAs) are among the most popular personal financial tools for working Americans. They benefit individuals in all income brackets. In fact, they may be the only tax shelter that millions of Americans with relatively modest incomes will ever use.

Insurance producers and financial practitioners who communicate to clients and prospects the privileges and responsibilities (as well as the many investment opportunities) that go along with IRA ownership provide a valuable service. Whether your main professional focus is insurance, securities, tax or financial planning, the information in this book will help you understand and explain IRAs better.

Our text will cover many topics related to IRAs as well as employer-sponsored simplified employee pension (SEP) programs, which are a form of IRA. We will discuss the history of the IRA from its initial availability in 1974 through today. Further, we will look at the rules that govern how money is put into IRAs (contributions) and the rules that affect how money comes out of IRAs (distributions)—and we'll look at the remarkable tax-free compounding that occurs in between these two important events.

Let's begin with a look at why IRAs were created, their advantages and the importance of retirement savings in general.

■ ■ ■ ■ ■

## ■ IRAs—A BRIEF HISTORY

The federal government has long recognized the importance of helping people save money for their retirement. By offering incentives to individuals and businesses to establish private savings and retirement plans, the government is able to transfer—at least in part—the responsibility for providing for one's old age onto the shoulders of private citizens and private enterprise.

The personal pension plan concept emerged in 1962 when Congress authorized *Keogh plans* for the self-employed. The goal was to give self-employed Americans an opportunity to establish tax-sheltered retirement plans in which invested money enjoys tax-free growth until it is withdrawn. Because the original Keogh rules were complex and restrictive, Keoghs did not gain popularity with self-employed business owners until 1974, when contribution limits were increased by 300 percent under a broad federal retirement plan law called the *Employee Retirement Income Security Act of 1974* (ERISA).

## ERISA and the First IRAs

ERISA also commissioned the first IRA program. The concept was simple: Permit individuals to deposit money into special accounts and then allow that money to grow tax-free until it is withdrawn at retirement. The accounts are set up through banks, investment firms and insurance companies that manage the investment and administration of the funds.

IRAs were intended to be a simple form of personal retirement plan for the average taxpayer. In fact, when they were first introduced, they were only available to workers who were not covered by an employer-sponsored or a union plan or who were ineligible to set up Keogh plans. The original law also included rollover provisions that would give employees who *were* covered by employer-provided plans "portability"—that is, the ability to move into an IRA the pension account value to which they were entitled, even if they and their employers had parted ways.

IRA contribution ceilings were *originally* set at $1,500 or 15 percent of income per year, whichever was less. Contributions were also fully tax deductible. In other words, if an individual was qualified to establish an IRA, the full amount of any contribution he or she made, up to the allowable ceiling, could be deducted for income-tax purposes.

The foundation established by ERISA was just the beginning. Since their introduction in 1974, IRAs have been subject to a myriad of legislative changes—some expansive, others restrictive—and it's likely that there are additional changes waiting on the horizon. A brief overview of this post-ERISA legislative history will help put today's IRA in a proper perspective.

### 1976—Tax Reform Act

The Tax Reform Act of 1976 created the *spousal IRA* that allowed an additional amount, up to $250, to be contributed to an IRA on behalf of a nonworking spouse. Thus, the overall limit was $1,750 for a worker and a nonworking spouse. To qualify for a spousal IRA, one spouse had to be a worker who was not participating in an employer-provided retirement plan, while the other had to be unemployed, with no earned income.

### 1978—Revenue Act

The Revenue Act of 1978 introduced *simplified employee pension* (SEP) plans. The intent of Congress in passing this legislation was to provide smaller employers with an opportunity to offer retirement benefits to their employees without the costs, paperwork and administrative burdens associated with traditional employer-sponsored qualified pension plans.

Essentially, a SEP plan allows an employer to establish and contribute to individual employee IRAs. Generally speaking, for other than contribution, deduction and reporting requirements, IRAs set up under an employer's SEP plan are governed by the same rules covering all other IRAs (which we will be discussing throughout this text). Because of this, SEPs are often referred to as "SEP-IRAs."

### 1981—Economic Recovery Tax Act

The Economic Recovery Tax Act, or ERTA, greatly expanded the availability and use of IRAs by allowing any working individual, regardless of whether he or she was covered by an employer plan, to establish and contribute to an IRA. In addition, the limit on annual contributions was increased to the lesser of $2,000 or 100 percent of compensation. This resulted in an explosion of IRA activity and popularity. Many people who were previously ineligible to open such accounts took advantage of the new universal nature of these retirement plans. For the next several years, financial professionals who sold products for the IRA market enjoyed high levels of production.

### 1984—Retirement Equity Act

The Retirement Equity Act redefined the term "compensation" to include taxable alimony and separate maintenance payments that are ordered by a court in connection with a divorce. (One of the requirements for being able to make IRA contributions is that individuals must have "earned compensation" as opposed to other forms of income.) Prior to this point, alimony did not qualify as "compensation"; thus, many divorced or legally separated nonworking spouses were unable to make contributions to IRAs. This liberalization of the law provided the greatest benefit to such nonworking spouses.

### 1986—Tax Reform Act

The tide expanding the scope of IRAs turned with the Tax Reform Act of 1986 (TRA '86). TRA '86 was a sweeping piece of legislation that affected many types of retirement plans, including IRAs. In fact, some practitioners felt that the "R" in TRA '86 stood for "ruination" rather than "reform," because the new restrictions put a damper on sales of retirement programs, especially IRAs.

TRA '86 drastically altered IRA rules by resurrecting the concept of "active participant" and by restricting the deductibility of IRA contributions. Whereas for many years prior to this law any working American could contribute to an IRA and deduct the full amount of that contribution, TRA '86 restricted deductions to (1) those who are not active participants in any employer-maintained retirement plan, and (2) those who are active participants but whose incomes fall below certain threshold levels. This change, combined with the fact that TRA '86 did not alter eligibility rules (virtually any working American can still open and contribute to an IRA) added a new dimension to IRAs: nondeductible contributions.

## IRAs Today—But Things Can Change

IRAs have undergone a number of changes since they were introduced two decades ago. Today, we could define an IRA as *a personal retirement savings arrangement under which eligible individuals can make both deductible and/or nondeductible contributions of up to $2,000 a year that grow tax free until further distributed.*

This definition highlights the important dimensions of IRAs and the rules by which they currently operate:

- *Personal retirement savings arrangement.* There are two types of IRAs—individual retirement accounts that may be funded by a variety of financial instruments and individual retirement annuities.

- *Eligible individuals.* Individuals eligible to establish an IRA are those under the age of 70½ with compensation. What does and does not qualify as "compensation" for IRA purposes is discussed in Chapter 3.

- *Deductible and/or nondeductible contributions up to $2,000 per year.* While an eligible individual may contribute to an IRA, the ability to deduct those contributions depends, in part, on whether the individual is an active participant in an employer-sponsored retirement plan and if so, the level of his or her income. Contributions and deductions are discussed in Chapter 3.

- *Grow tax-free.* All IRA contributions, deductible and nondeductible, accumulate on a tax-deferred basis, which greatly enhances their growth. This is one of the primary advantages of an IRA and will be discussed in Chapter 3.

- *Until distributed.* IRAs are designed to be long-term savings programs; consequently, there are rules governing how and when funds may be distributed. These rules are discussed in Chapter 6.

As our brief history of IRAs indicates, things change. A number of bills have recently been introduced in Congress to liberalize IRA contribution deductibility, raise contribution limits and even allow withdrawals from IRAs without penalty by individuals under the normal penalty age of 59½ for reasons such as educational expenses, first-time home purchase and certain types of financial "hardship." There appears to be bipartisan support for IRA reform. The financial practitioner should be alert to new IRA developments that may be on the horizon.

## ■ ADVANTAGES OF IRAs

Despite the many changes and restrictions imposed on IRAs in recent years, they remain a great way for individuals to save for retirement. IRAs have many advantages, from tax-free growth to investment flexibility.

### Tax-Free Growth

An IRA shelters interest, dividends and capital gains earnings until IRA owners are ready to start withdrawing their money. To avoid "premature withdrawal" penalties, withdrawals may be made at any time between the ages of 59½ and April 1 of the year following the year in which the owner of the IRA becomes 70½. (By the age of 70½, the owner *must* begin withdrawing at least part of his or her IRA money.) Of course, the longer an IRA's tax-sheltered earnings keep compounding, the larger the fund will be when it is time for the IRA owner to retire.

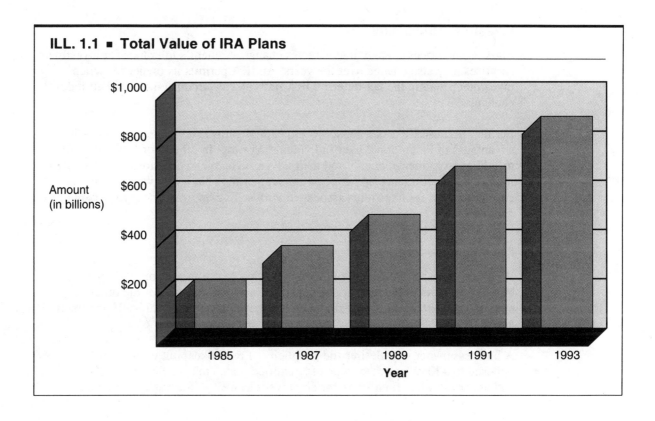

**ILL. 1.1 ■ Total Value of IRA Plans**

### Clients Control Their IRAs

An IRA is completely under the control of the IRA owner. With the benefit of sound advice from his or her financial adviser, the IRA owner decides how to invest the money contributed to the account. The owner can also decide whether to save his or her IRA money for retirement or use it sooner (though penalties may apply for IRA withdrawals by individuals under age 59½). No matter how often IRA owners change jobs, their IRAs are always in place. As a result, IRAs may be especially appropriate for your clients who change jobs frequently.

### IRAs Enhance Diversification Opportunities

IRAs give your clients an opportunity to further diversify their investments. Though IRAs generally can't hold hard assets, such as real estate properties, or collectibles, such as antiques or diamonds, most other investments are permitted in an IRA. Therefore, IRA investments can complement other investments that may not be in an ideal market position to sell when retirement income is needed.

### Annual Contributions Not Required

IRA owners don't have to make contributions to their IRAs every year if they don't want to or can't afford to. The IRS cares more about the maximum annual contribution limits; it does not insist on any annual minimum deposit. (However, you should be aware that certain investments or custodians may require certain minimum deposits even though the IRS does not.)

## Investment Flexibility

Markets and prices change. Interest rates change. A client's tolerance for investment surprises may also change over the years. An IRA permits its owner to switch investments within the tax-deferred IRA umbrella as circumstances and attitudes change.

Further, because IRAs are not subject to capital gains taxes, investors enjoy the tax advantages of institutional over individual investing. In other words, when it comes to selling investments, clients and their advisers can make decisions based solely on investment performance and expectations rather than having to worry about the current income-tax exposures associated with selling an investment for a capital gain or loss.

## IRAs Can "Discriminate"

If an IRA owner is a business owner who wishes to set up a Keogh or other type of business retirement plan, he or she generally has to contribute for the other employees. With an IRA, a business owner may contribute for himself or herself alone.

A business owner who desires the simplicity of recordkeeping with an IRA, as opposed to a Keogh or other type of "qualified plan," may establish a SEP program and under this plan, fund IRAs for employees as well as for himself or herself.

## Deductions Still Widely Available

Individuals who are not covered under an employer-provided retirement plan may still deduct their entire annual IRA contribution. This category, which is larger than many financial practitioners realize, includes those who simply do not have *any* available employer-sponsored retirement plan whatsoever. Moreover, if their incomes fall under certain threshold amounts, some of your clients who *are* covered under employer-sponsored retirement plans may still be able to deduct their IRA contributions, fully or in part. This deduction can reduce their tax bill each year.

For example, Elizabeth, a free-lance public relations writer in the 28 percent marginal (federal) income tax bracket, earns $50,000 in a particular tax year. Other than owning an IRA, Elizabeth does not participate in any retirement plan. She decides to contribute $2,000 to her IRA for that same year. Because Elizabeth is not covered by another retirement plan, her $2,000 contribution is entirely deductible. Based on her 28 percent tax bracket, Elizabeth's deductible IRA contribution represents a $560 reduction in her tax bill—not a poor reward for saving for her *own* retirement!

## IRAs Cushion the Downside of Forced Retirement

In the current corporate environment, with its frequent "downsizing" and "rightsizing," more and more workers are being forced or influenced into retiring early. In other cases, health problems may force clients to retire earlier than they intended. With money in their IRAs, your clients will be better prepared for retirement if it is forced on them earlier than originally planned.

### Great Flexibility after Age 59½

IRAs provide their owners with great flexibility to adapt to changes in their particular financial and employment circumstances during the important years between 59½ and 70½ (i.e., the years during which IRA funds may be withdrawn without penalty and before they are required to be withdrawn). If your clients over age 59½ are still earning compensation, they may continue to make IRA contributions during those years, even though they are also making withdrawals.

### IRAs Can Provide Income for a Lifetime

If IRAs are used to provide retirement income, their payout can be designed to produce an income stream that the IRA owner cannot outlive. This is accomplished by *annuitizing* the distributions, which will be discussed in more detail in Chapter 6.

### IRAs Can Be Inherited by Anyone

An IRA can be inherited by one or more people in the event that the owner dies before the money in the account is fully distributed. If an individual chooses to name his or her spouse as the beneficiary and the IRA owner dies before distributions from his or her IRA start, then the spouse may delay taking distributions—and paying the tax—until the year when the original account owner would have reached 70½. Otherwise, the spouse may choose to roll over the account to his or her own IRA.

## ■ THE IMPORTANCE OF RETIREMENT SAVINGS

A typical individual may begin saving for retirement beginning at age 30, retire at age 65 and enjoy retirement until age 85. During these 55 years of retirement savings and distribution, inflation steadily reduces the buying power of every retirement dollar, year after year.

When McDonald's first appeared in American neighborhoods, it cost roughly 15 cents to buy a simple hamburger. Today, that same burger costs about 69 cents. Fifteen cents no longer buys lunch. Economists develop complex theories about inflation, but in the real world, inflation is about hamburgers—and your client's standard of living during retirement. Even a "low" rate of inflation can destroy buying power over an extended time period.

As inflation erodes buying power, living standards fall, particularly for your clients who must depend on fixed retirement incomes (such as those from defined benefit pension plans or fixed annuities) or on retirement incomes that do not rise as much as the inflation rate.

### How IRAs Fight Inflation

Because IRA earnings compound tax deferred, owners have a good opportunity to increase the actual purchasing power of the assets in their IRAs. During periods of high inflation, the IRA has a much better chance of maintaining purchasing power relative to nontax-sheltered investments. During periods of relatively low inflation, its purchasing power should actually *grow*.

When building an IRA, individuals and financial practitioners should keep trying to earn a return that outperforms the rate at which prices are rising in general—that is, the inflation rate. For many years it was difficult for most people to earn more than the inflation rate with their savings because of ceilings on the interest paid by banks and thrift institutions, but now there are no rate ceilings on savings instruments at such institutions, and they can pay savers at rates that reflect prevailing demand for interest.

In the United States, the rate at which the prices of goods and services rise or fall is measured by the Consumer Price Index (CPI). The Bureau of Labor Statistics reports the CPI every month. While the CPI is not a perfect measure of inflation, it is the best yardstick available. There can be big swings in the monthly CPI rate for any number of reasons, such as weather problems or political unrest.

If the CPI rate is occasionally higher than the rate that your clients' IRAs are earning, there's nothing to worry about. And there may be periods—thankfully not too many—when inflation is rising so fast that it is outpacing virtually all investments. But if the CPI rate is consistently higher than the return on your clients' IRAs, consider switching all or a portion of that retirement money to investments that offer higher returns.

## Comparing IRA Returns against Taxable Returns

Because an IRA shelters investment earnings from immediate taxation, one approach to determining its value as an investment is to compare its return versus the *taxable-equivalent return* on investments that are not shelters. A taxable-equivalent return is what a taxable investment must yield to make that investment equal to the IRA.

Taxable equivalent returns will vary among your clients, based upon their different (marginal) income-tax brackets. Equivalent returns on IRAs are usually significantly higher than what an investor could expect to enjoy without the tax-deferred growth associated with IRAs.

For example, if a person's IRA earns 10 percent and he or she is in the 28 percent tax bracket, he or she would have to receive the equivalent of a 13.9 percent return on a taxable investment to equal the IRA. An IRA owner in the 33 percent tax bracket would have to receive a taxable equivalent return of 14.9 percent.

## How Large Can an IRA Grow?

The wonder of an IRA is that it combines years of tax sheltering with years of compounded returns. An IRA's capital-building potential is greatest for people in their twenties and thirties. For example, Sally, a 25-year-old, invests $2,000 at the start of each year in an IRA earning 10 percent annually. At age 59½, her IRA will be worth $567,482. At age 65, the account will be worth $973,704. And at age 70½, when Sally must begin taking distributions from the IRA, her account will be worth seven figures: $1,659,860.

Obviously, starting an IRA in later years will produce lower results, but not necessarily shabby ones. For example, take Paul, an investor earning 10 percent who

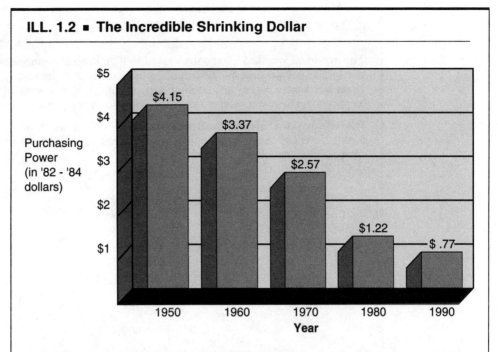

## ILL. 1.2 ■ The Incredible Shrinking Dollar

Using the Consumer Price Index to reflect inflation over a period of 40 years, this chart shows the purchasing power of a dollar as measured in 1982–1984 dollars. In 1950, a single dollar would buy $4.15 worth of goods (in 1982–1984 dollars). By 1990, that single dollar bought about 77 cents worth of goods. It's clear that a sound investment strategy is necessary just to keep pace with (let alone outstrip) inflation.

starts his IRA at age 40. By depositing $2,000 a year, he will have a fund worth $119,117 at age 59½; $216,364 at age 65; and $380,624 at age 70½.

Don't assume that it's too late for your fifty-something clients to become first-time IRA investors. For instance, if Roger, a 55-year-old, also invested $2,000 a year in an IRA earning 10 percent annually, he will have $11,782 in his account at age 59½; $35,062 at age 65; and $74,385 at age 70½.

### The Power of Compounding

The strength of the IRA as a personal financial miracle is that all of its interest, dividends and capital gains are sheltered from current taxation. It's impossible to predict where interest rates will be in the future. However, consider this: if an IRA earns a constant 7 percent compounded annually, after only 10 years a total $20,000 investment ($2,000 annual contributions are assumed) would be worth $27,632, a $7,632 gain; after 20 years, the $40,000 invested would be worth $81,990; in 30 years, the $60,000 invested would be worth $188,921; and in 40 years, the total $80,000 invested would be worth $399,270. (Contributions of $2,000 each by working couples would double the figures.)

### ILL. 1.3 ■ IRA Tax-Free Accumulation

If an individual invests $2,000 each year in an IRA, interest earnings accumulate tax free and do not increase the individual's gross income until the savings are withdrawn. There is a sizable benefit to contributing the maximum annual amount because compounding of interest can dramatically increase savings over a long period of time.

The following chart shows how the balance of an IRA increases with consistent contributions and tax-free accumulation (assumed interest rate of 6 percent compounded annually).

| Current Age | Total Deposited by Age 65 ($2,000 per year) | IRA Value at Age 65 |
|---|---|---|
| 30 | $70,000 | $222,870 |
| 35 | 60,000 | 158,116 |
| 40 | 50,000 | 109,729 |
| 45 | 40,000 | 73,571 |
| 50 | 30,000 | 46,551 |
| 55 | 20,000 | 26,361 |
| 60 | 10,000 | 11,274 |

## How Much Retirement Income Can an IRA Produce?

As we will discuss later in this book, IRA funds cannot be sheltered indefinitely. The law requires that distributions begin no later than April 1 following the year the IRA owner turns 70½. However, even after your clients are required to start withdrawing their money from their IRAs, the money that remains in the account continues to grow tax deferred.

If your clients have enough income and don't need to use the money from their IRAs for living expenses, they can reinvest the money they must take out after they are required to begin making withdrawals. If tax minimization is a concern, tax-advantaged investments, including fixed and variable annuities or municipal bonds, may be selected.

However, most people will count on their IRAs as an additional source of retirement income. How much income an IRA will generate during retirement (or before, if a client needs income sooner) will depend on the value of the IRA, the rate of return and the length of time the IRA is expected to provide income. Obviously, larger IRAs will produce correspondingly larger amounts of retirement income.

Calculating an IRA's retirement income can help your clients determine the amount of savings that they will need to retire comfortably. Like all phases of life, retirement begins with realistic objectives and plans to achieve those objectives. By projecting the potential income generated by an IRA, your clients can have a clearer understanding of the time value of money.

## ■ SUMMARY

Today, IRAs are among the best personal financial planning tools available to Americans. Despite years of legislative changes, IRAs are still considered excellent retirement investing vehicles.

IRA owners enjoy tax-deferred compounding, investment freedom and flexibility as well as many other advantages. A program of regular IRA contributions, started early in one's working life, can produce a significant source of retirement income. Also, careful planning of IRA distributions can maximize overall returns from IRAs.

In the next chapter, we'll look at the various types of IRAs, as well as different IRA investment providers.

## ■ CHAPTER 1 QUESTIONS FOR REVIEW

1. Which of the statements below best describes the impact of the Tax Reform Act of 1986 (TRA '86) on IRAs?

    a. After TRA '86, few Americans could make an IRA contribution.
    b. After TRA '86, fewer Americans could deduct IRA contributions.
    c. After TRA '86, contribution limits would be adjusted to account for annual inflation.
    d. After TRA '86, all working Americans could deduct annual IRA contributions.

2. All of the following are advantages to IRA ownership EXCEPT

    a. tax-deferred compounding.
    b. unlimited annual contributions.
    c. investment flexibility.
    d. right to name a beneficiary.

3. Which of the following are tax deferred within an IRA?

    a. Dividends
    b. Interest
    c. Capital gains
    d. All of the above

4. When may an IRA owner have access to his or her IRA funds?

    a. Only after age 59½
    b. At any time, although penalties may apply
    c. Only after age 70½
    d. At any time, if the specified beneficiary consents in writing

5. IRAs should generally be regarded as

   a. short-term tax shelters.
   b. controlled largely by employers.
   c. long-term retirement investments.
   d. cash values from which borrowing is easily available.

6. Which of the following is the most widely regarded measure of inflation?

   a. Gross National Product (GNP)
   b. Balance of Payments (BOP)
   c. Consumer Price Index (CPI)
   d. Implicit Price Index (IPI)

7. Which of the following factors should generally produce larger IRA account values?

   a. Beginning to fund an IRA at a younger age
   b. Generally earning rates of return that are higher than the rate of inflation
   c. Neither a nor b
   d. Both a and b

# 2

## IRA Types and Investment Providers

**M**ost Americans are familiar with how the basic IRA works: a person independently deposits money, up to $2,000 annually, into a retirement account that's offered by a financial institution, such as a bank or mutual fund. Yet, there are several other types of IRA arrangements with which many Americans (and even some financial representatives) may be less familiar.

This chapter will begin by exploring various types of IRAs, including regular IRAs, IRA annuities, IRAs established by businesses and other entities (rather than by individuals), as well as spousal and inherited IRAs.

In addition, we'll compare different IRA investment providers including banks, which typically offer certificates of deposit (CDs); brokerage houses, which offer a wide range of securities and mutual funds; and life insurance companies, which offer both fixed and variable annuities.

■ ■ ■ ■ ■

### ■ IRAs—MORE THAN ONE TYPE

By definition, an individual retirement account is a *trust* or *custodial account* set up in the United States for the exclusive benefit of an individual taxpayer and his or her beneficiaries. According to the IRS, the account is actually created by means of a written IRA document. The IRS requires this document to demonstrate that the IRA satisfies all of the following requirements:

- The account must have a trustee or custodian. This custodian must be a bank, a federally insured credit union, a savings and loan association or an entity approved by the IRS to serve as a trustee or custodian (insurance and securities companies generally fall into this category).

- The trustee or custodian generally cannot accept contributions greater than $2,000 per individual account, per year. However, rollover contributions and employer contributions to simplified employee pensions (SEPs) can be more than $2,000.

- Contributions that do not involve rollovers must be in cash, which includes checks or money orders.

- The taxpayer must be fully vested in the amount in his or her IRA. This means that the account owner has a nonforfeitable right to the total assets in his or her account at all times.

- Money in the taxpayer's account cannot be used to buy a life insurance policy.

- Assets in an IRA cannot be combined with other personal assets.

- The taxpayer must begin receiving at least partial distributions from his or her account no later than April 1 of the year following the year when he or she turns 70½.

With these seven requirements for an IRA in mind, let's look at the various types of IRAs available.

## Individual Retirement Annuities

An *individual retirement annuity* is established by purchasing an annuity contract or an endowment contract from a life insurance company in compliance with certain standards and guidelines.

Annuities are purchased through the payment of premiums to an insurance company. Only the annuity owner and the beneficiaries who survive that owner may receive payments from the annuity. The IRS has a list of individual retirement annuity requirements:

- The owner's entire interest in the annuity account must be nonforfeitable.

- The owner may not transfer any portion of the annuity to any party other than the issuer (e.g., the life insurance company).

- Annuity contracts issued after November 6, 1978, must provide for flexible payment of premiums. The thought behind this requirement is that if an owner's compensation changes from year to year, contributions to the individual retirement annuity must also be able to change accordingly.

- The owner cannot contribute more than $2,000 per year to his or her individual retirement annuity. In addition, any refunded premiums must be used to pay for future premiums or to buy more benefits before the end of the calendar year when the owner receives the refund. This requirement minimizes the potential for "accidental" premature distributions.

- The annuity must begin distributions by April 1 of the year following the year when the owner reaches age 70½.

### Rollover IRAs

An *IRA rollover* involves a tax-free distribution of cash or other assets from one retirement program to another. Rollover contributions to IRAs may come from other IRAs or from qualified retirement plans established by the IRA owner's employer or former employer.

Rollover accounts are *not* subject to the $2,000 annual contribution limits that are associated with regular IRAs. We will examine IRA rollovers and transfers in greater detail in Chapter 4.

### Employer and Employee Association Trust Accounts

An employer, labor union or other employee association may establish a trust to provide IRAs for its employees or members. The rules for IRAs also apply to employer and employee association trust accounts.

### Simplified Employee Pensions

A *simplified employee pension* (SEP) is a written arrangement that permits certain employers to make deductible contributions to an employee's IRA, which is generally referred to as a SEP-IRA. SEPs will be discussed at greater length in Chapter 5.

### Spousal IRAs

As you will recall from Chapter 1, an IRA owner may be able to establish and contribute to an IRA for his or her spouse, regardless of whether the spouse received compensation in the taxable year. This arrangement is known as a *spousal IRA*.

However, an individual cannot set up an IRA that is co-owned with the spouse. The IRA owner and spouse must maintain *separate* IRAs. An individual who has already established an IRA who later wishes to set one up for his or her spouse may keep the existing IRA and start another one for the spouse.

To contribute to a spousal IRA, several requirements must be met:

- The IRA owner and spouse must be married at the end of the tax year for which the spousal contribution is being made.

- The IRA owner and spouse must file a joint tax return (married, filing jointly) for the tax year that corresponds to the spousal contribution.

- The spouse on whose behalf the contribution is being made must be under age 70½ at the end of the tax year when the spousal contribution applies.

- The contributing spouse must have taxable compensation for the applicable year, while the noncontributing spouse must either have no compensation or if eligible compensation is less than $250, choose to be treated as having no compensation for the tax year.

### Inherited IRAs

IRAs can be inherited just like any other property. Beneficiaries, however, must observe special rules.

Nonspousal beneficiaries may not make contributions (including rollover contributions) to the inherited IRA, nor may they roll the account over into another type of noninherited account to receive more favorable tax treatment. However, nonspousal beneficiaries still enjoy the same tax deferrals as do other IRA owners. In most cases, there is no federal income tax liability on the assets in the IRA until the beneficiary actually receives distributions from it.

Spousal beneficiaries have more options. A beneficiary who is a surviving spouse may elect to treat an inherited IRA as his or her own. Thus, he or she can make contributions, including rollover contributions, to the inherited IRA.

## ■ IRA INVESTMENT PROVIDERS

IRAs can be established with several types of organizations. Most banks, savings and loan associations, mutual funds, stock brokerage firms and insurance companies offer IRAs that satisfy the Internal Revenue Code's various requirements.

How does a consumer decide which organization to use in setting up an IRA?

The choice of organization will be based, in part, on an individual's investment preference for funding the IRA. For example, someone preferring an individual retirement annuity is more likely to establish his or her IRA with an insurance company while an individual preferring stocks may choose to set up his or her IRA with a stock brokerage firm or a mutual fund.

### Banks

*Banks* may limit their investment alternatives for IRA accounts to fixed-rate and variable-rate certificates of deposit, passbook accounts and money-market deposit accounts. These investments are protected by FDIC insurance, up to $100,000 per person, per bank. The fees, if any, charged for opening and maintaining an IRA are relatively small.

Commercial banks may also market and manage common funds for IRA customers, giving them a wider range of investment choices and flexibility. They may also provide other conveniences, such as transfers from checking accounts and direct payroll deductions.

Today you may find securities representatives operating within the premises of their banks. Because of prohibitions against banks operating as securities brokerages, securities desks within banks often represent an entity separate from the bank.

### Brokerage Houses

Through "self-directed" IRAs, *brokerage houses* offer the widest range of investment alternatives. Some offer everything from money-market funds and stocks and bonds to limited partnership interests in real estate and other endeavors.

---

ILL. 2.1 *Investment Choices When Interest Rates Are Low*

IRA contributions should not be delayed in anticipation of higher interest rates. However, investment choices should be made with potential higher interest rate opportunities in mind. The earlier an IRA contribution is made, the sooner earnings on the contribution begin to accrue on a tax-deferred basis. In turn, this leads to a greater compounding of interest which, over the life of the IRA, can mean thousands of extra dollars.

Investors who anticipate a rise in interest rates may consider nonfixed investments for the short run, such as money market funds or market deposit accounts. When interest rates increase, the money can be switched to a higher-yielding fixed vehicle such as a certificate of deposit.

---

Fees to open and maintain IRAs in brokerage houses are generally higher than with other IRA providers. Some may charge a fee based on the number of separate investments held within the account, while others may charge a fee that relates to the dollar value of the account. To attract larger IRA rollover business, some brokerages waive or reduce fees for accounts over a certain amount.

Some brokerage houses suggest that a different IRA investment be selected each year to foster investment diversification and thus provide the relative safety and stability that's generally associated with diversification. As long as the self-directed IRA owner maintains the same brokerage house as custodian, he or she may move IRA assets among different investments to enhance diversification or to pursue the best return. This offers a significant advantage over investing in bank certificates where an investor may be unable to dispose of the investment without facing interest penalties.

Brokerage-provided, self-directed IRA accounts do *not* offer the guaranteed return or safety that accompanies bank deposits, but if the account is invested in U.S. government securities, it does enjoy the "full faith and credit" of the federal government.

## IRA Investment Options

IRA owners have numerous options available to them when it comes to investing their savings. From stocks and bonds to mutual funds, IRA owners can make investment choices depending on their current needs and long-term goals.

### Stocks

*Stocks* are units of ownership in corporations that have historically provided a much better hedge against inflation than debt securities, such as bonds.

### Zero-Coupon Bonds

*Zero-coupon bonds* may appeal to investors in IRAs and other tax-deferred retirement accounts because they virtually eliminate the problem of reinvesting interest payments at lower rates of return if interest rates fall (assuming that the bonds are held to maturity).

A zero-coupon bond derives its name from the simple fact that the bond is issued with a 0 percent coupon rate. The return on a zero-coupon bond comes from the gradual increase in the bond's price from the discount to face value, which it reaches at maturity.

Investors should be aware that any zero-coupon bond's absence of current income makes it more volatile than interest-bearing bonds.

Certain zero-coupon bonds are based on underlying U.S. Treasury issues. They are often marketed by brokerage houses under names associated with animals. Examples include CATs (certificates of accrual on Treasury securities) or COUGARS (certificates on government receipts). An investor who is buying one of these is not really buying the Treasury security itself. Rather, the investor acquires a receipt entitling him or her to the value of a Treasury security held in escrow.

The government directly issues zero-coupon Treasuries through its securities called STRIPS (separate trading of registered interest and principal of securities). Because they have direct government backing and avoid complicated trust arrangements, STRIPS yield a little less interest than other government-backed zero securities.

## Mutual Funds

*Mutual funds* are popular choices for IRA accounts, because they offer a wide range of investment alternatives. There are families of mutual funds ranging from conservative to very aggressive growth and enhanced yield funds. The IRA investor may move from one fund to another without tax or transfer consequences, as long as the move is within the same fund family and involves the same custodian or trustee. Typically, investors in a family of funds can transfer assets (usually for a minimal fee) with just a phone call or by filling out a few forms.

Minimum contributions to set up an IRA at most mutual funds range from $25 to $500, while subsequent contributions to add to an IRA are usually for smaller amounts. Some funds also arrange to have withdrawals made automatically from your clients' checking accounts and placed into your clients' IRAs.

A major advantage of mutual funds is that they offer significant diversification for a small investment. If an IRA owner invests $2,000 in a common stock fund, then he or she can typically buy a piece of 80 or 90 companies.

### The Fund's Prospectus

Every mutual fund states its financial objective clearly in its *prospectus*. Before your client may invest in a mutual fund, he or she must be presented with a copy of the fund's prospectus.

Although the prospectus may be intimidating reading material, the IRA owner should be encouraged to read it. The prospectus provides the IRA owner with the necessary information to understand the mutual fund's objectives. The IRA owner can then decide whether the fund's investment goals are compatible with his or her own financial goals.

For example, suppose you have a client who is nearing retirement and who will depend on the IRA as the major source of retirement income. This client may wish to avoid mutual funds that emphasize speculative investments that pay little or no dividends and may not enjoy capital gains for years.

A prospectus also reveals the specific investments in the fund's portfolio. It should also disclose all fees charged by the fund.

### Types of Mutual Funds

There are many different types of mutual funds that your client can select. The most popular are:

- *Diversified common stock funds.* These funds invest in a wide variety of common stocks in many different industries. Their emphasis can range from moderate income with moderate capital growth and relatively good stability of principal ("blue-chip funds") to minimal income with maximum capital growth and little stability of principal ("aggressive growth funds"). Aggressive growth funds typically invest in relatively small companies that are in growing industries.

- *Bond funds.* These funds invest in debt instruments with initial maturities exceeding one year. Bond funds may further describe themselves as investing primarily in either corporate debt securities or in U.S. government and agency securities.

- *Money-market funds.* Money-market funds invest in short-term debt instruments, such as Treasury bills, negotiable certificates of deposit, bankers acceptances, commercial paper and Eurodollars. Money-market funds, except in periods of high inflation, have provided relatively modest returns, perhaps in exchange for very high liquidity.

- *Asset allocation funds.* These funds invest in stocks, bonds, money-market instruments and other investments such as precious metals and real estate. Allocation among the categories is determined by the fund's managers who may try to time allocations based on interest rates and their predictions of movements in the stock market.

- *Index funds.* These funds attempt to duplicate the performance of a commonly followed stock market indicator such as Standard & Poor's 500 Index or the NYSE Composite Index. The objective is to create a portfolio that has the same securities in the same proportions as the index. Index funds reflect the belief that outperforming the market on a risk-adjusted basis is virtually impossible.

- *Sector funds.* These funds invest primarily in the common stock of a single industry. These include financial services, gold-oriented, health/biotechnology, real estate, science and technology, and utility industries. Although diversified among various companies within one industry, the lack of diversification among industries makes sector funds riskier than more diversified funds.

### Insurance Companies

The insurance industry's basic IRA product is the flexible premium annuity, which may be either fixed or variable. With a fixed annuity, your clients are guaranteed a maximum rate of return for the first one to five years and then a minimum rate of return thereafter. Typically, the written minimum guaranteed return over a long-term period is low. Today it's around 4 percent.

Fixed IRA annuities provide safety and stability and reasonable rates of return relative to their risk. However, returns may be lower than those of other investments. Although fixed annuities are vulnerable to inflation, retirement income from an insurance annuity does have the advantage of being guaranteed. Your clients do not have to worry over loss of retirement income because of the ups and downs of the economy.

With variable annuities, your client is given a choice of several different investment portfolios. Just as with a family of mutual funds, your client can switch from one fund to another without a rollover or transfer. Usually, an insurance company group will include one or more common stock funds, a money-market fund and a bond or fixed-income fund.

Charges and fees vary greatly among insurance companies offering IRA annuities. Today most annuity companies have adopted "back-load" charges that will be assessed if your clients withdraw their money before a specific time period has elapsed, usually from seven to ten years. These "withdrawal charges" decline each year the annuity contract is held until they eventually disappear.

### Collectibles

The Internal Revenue Code penalizes an IRA owner who directs his or her investments into collectibles. Examples of collectibles include artwork, rugs, antiques, metals, gems, stamps, rare books, coins and any other tangible personal property characterized as such by the IRS. The Internal Revenue Code provides that if any IRA assets are used to acquire a collectible, the amount is treated as a distribution, which is therefore taxable to the owner.

However, IRAs are permitted to invest in certain U.S. Treasury-minted gold and silver coins, including one-ounce, half-ounce, quarter-ounce and tenth-of-an-ounce gold bullion coins and a one-ounce silver bullion coin. Coins issued by states are also permissible IRA investments.

### ■ SUMMARY

As we have seen in this chapter, besides regular IRAs, there are several other types of IRAs available to the consumer: annuities, rollover, spousal, employee association trust accounts and SEPs.

There are also different types of financial providers that offer a wide variety of IRA investment choices. Banks offer a limited number of insured vehicles, including certificates of deposit, passbook accounts and money-market deposit accounts. Brokerage firms offer stocks, interest-bearing bonds and zero-coupon bonds as well as mutual funds. Insurance companies offer both fixed and variable IRA annuity contracts.

IRA investment choices are ultimately determined by the needs—and goals—of your clients. By understanding the strengths and weaknesses of various IRA investment accounts, you can help your clients decide which IRA is best suited for their retirement needs.

## ■ CHAPTER 2 QUESTIONS FOR REVIEW

1. Assuming that this is not a rollover, which of the following may be accepted by an IRA custodian?

   a. $3,000 in cash
   b. $5,000 worth of readily traded stocks
   c. $2,000 in cash
   d. $1,000 worth of Treasury bonds

2. Hal and May Wilson, a married couple, file their income taxes jointly. Because May does not work outside the home, Hal plans to establish and fund an IRA for his wife. This arrangement is best described as a

   a. joint IRA.
   b. joint and last survivor IRA.
   c. spousal IRA.
   d. marital deduction IRA.

3. The widest range of IRA investment alternatives is generally provided by

   a. brokerage houses.
   b. federal and state banks.
   c. international mutual funds.
   d. fixed annuity issuers.

4. Which of the following is a characteristic of a fixed IRA annuity contract?

   a. Inflation protection
   b. Safety of principal
   c. High investor participation
   d. Values quoted in the daily financial press

5. All of the following investments are permissible in an IRA EXCEPT

   a. bond funds.
   b. U.S.-minted, half-ounce gold coins.
   c. a $10,000 Oriental rug.
   d. Eurodollars.

# 3

# IRA Contributions and Deductions

T here have been so many changes and proposed changes regarding the rules for IRAs that many people are confused as to whether they can make a contribution to an IRA and whether they can deduct their contribution on their income-tax forms.

This chapter takes a close look at the rules governing IRA contributions and deductions. Specifically, we'll describe the various contribution limits and timing restrictions that apply to IRAs.

■ ■ ■ ■ ■

## ■ IRA CONTRIBUTIONS

As soon as a regular, nonrollover IRA is set up, the IRA owner may make contributions to his or her IRA account through a custodian, trustee or other administrator. Contributions must be in the form of money: only cash, checks or money orders will be accepted by IRA custodians. An individual may not contribute property, including investments, to a regular IRA. (Although the law allows rollover IRAs to accept property as well as cash, many IRA plan documents don't accept any contributions in the form of property.)

Individuals can make contributions to their IRAs each year that they qualify for an IRA. Even if an IRA owner doesn't qualify to make contributions for the current year, the amounts contributed for years in which he or she did qualify can, of course, remain in an IRA.

To "qualify," an IRA owner must have received "taxable compensation" as defined by the Internal Revenue Code. Typically, this is what your clients earn from working—that is, their yearly compensation. The rule regarding taxable compensation applies regardless of whether the contribution is deductible.

## What Income Is Compensation?

The IRS treats any amount shown (factoring reductions for certain nonqualified plans) in Box 1 of a taxpayer's W-2 form as compensation. According to the IRS, compensation includes:

- wages;

- salaries;

- tips;

- professional fees;

- bonuses;

- commissions; and

- other amounts received for providing personal services.

### Self-Employment Income

If an IRA owner is self-employed in the role of a sole proprietor or partner, compensation is considered the net earnings from his or her trade or business if the services materially contribute to the income of the business. (Income earned as a "silent partner" would *not* be included as compensation. If an IRA owner invests in a partnership but does not provide services that are a material income-producing factor to the partnership, his or her share of partnership income will not be treated as compensation for IRA purposes.)

Today, more and more individuals hold jobs with companies as well as operate their own small businesses. When individuals have both self-employment income and salaries and wages, the IRS will consider compensation to be the sum of those amounts. Sometimes, however, an IRA owner may have a net loss from operating his or her own businesses. When this occurs, an IRA owner should *not* subtract the loss amount from salaries or wages received when calculating total compensation.

### Alimony and Separate Maintenance

All taxable alimony and separate maintenance income that an individual receives under a divorce or separate maintenance decree is treated as compensation. If an individual receives taxable alimony but does not work, it's still possible for him or her to make an eligible IRA contribution.

## Contribution Limits

The most that an individual can contribute for any single year to a regular IRA is the lesser of:

- 100 percent of the IRA owner's compensation that was included for federal income tax reporting or

- $2,000.

---

**ILL. 3.1  *What Income Is Not Compensation?***

**F**or IRA purposes, the following is *not* considered compensation by the IRS:

* earnings from property, such as rental income, interest income and dividend income;

* pension and annuity income;

* any deferred compensation received (compensation amounts postponed from a past year);

* foreign-earned income and housing cost amounts that are excluded from taxable income; and

* any other amounts that are excluded from taxable income.

---

The yearly contribution limits do *not* change when an individual maintains more than one IRA, nor are these limits influenced by whether the contribution is deductible.

If your clients' contributions to their IRAs for a given year were less than the smaller of 100 percent of their compensation or $2,000, they can't contribute more in a later year to make up the difference. Unfortunately, the IRS does not allow retroactive or cumulative IRA contribution limits.

Also, brokerage commissions that individuals pay in conjunction with their IRAs neither increase the annual contribution limit nor are they deductible.

Trustee or custodian administrative and reporting fees that are billed to an IRA owner are *not* subject to the contribution limit. To avoid confusion, however, your clients may wish to use a separate check for their annual IRA contribution and another for their annual IRA maintenance fee. Under certain circumstances, the taxpayer may be able to deduct these fees as a miscellaneous deduction.

### Spousal IRA Contribution Limits

The total contribution limit that can be made to a working individual's IRA combined with a spousal IRA for that individual's nonworking spouse is the lesser of:

* 100 percent of the working spouse's compensation for the year or

* $2,250 a year.

With a spousal IRA, contributions can be divided between the working spouse's IRA and the nonworking spouse's IRA in any manner the working spouse chooses—as long as no more than $2,000 is contributed to either IRA. IRA owners are not required to make contributions to their own IRAs or to spousal IRAs for every tax year, even if they have the financial means to do so.

If both the IRA owner and his or her spouse have taxable compensation during the year and both are under age 70½ at the end of the year, both the IRA owner and the spouse can each have regular (rather than one regular and one spousal) IRAs. Each

---

> ### ILL. 3.2 *IRA Contribution Limits*
>
> The following examples illustrate IRA contribution limits:
>
> - Martin, who is single, earned $23,000 this year. His IRA contribution for this year would be limited to $2,000.
> - Alice, who attends the local community college and works part-time, earned $1,800 this year. Her IRA contribution for this year would be limited to $1,800, or 100 percent of her compensation.

may contribute up to 100 percent of his or her eligible compensation up to the $2,000 limit.

However, if the spouse has eligible compensation that amounts to less than $250, he or she can choose to be treated as having *no* compensation and use the rules for spousal IRAs that generally apply to nonworking spouses. In most cases, if one spouse has compensation of less than $250 for the year, and the couple wishes to maximize their combined contributions, a spousal IRA is a smarter move than having two regular IRAs.

When both your client and his or her spouse receive compensation, each one can set up an IRA. However, both spouses cannot participate in the same IRA—there is no such thing as a "joint" IRA. The maximum contribution for each spouse's IRA is calculated separately and depends on how much each spouse earned in the applicable year.

Although certain states that maintain community property laws may combine earnings of spouses for some legal and tax purposes, the IRS does not take community property laws into consideration when it comes to IRAs. Even in community property states, however, each spouse's maximum annual regular IRA contribution is factored separately.

In situations where a spouse inherits an IRA from a spouse, he or she can choose to treat it as personally owned and make contributions to the inherited IRA. However, as already stated, nonspousal beneficiaries cannot treat inherited IRAs as personally owned and subsequently are prohibited by the IRS from adding contributions to the inherited IRA.

### When to Contribute

Individuals can make contributions to their own IRAs (or to spousal IRAs) for a given year any time during that year or by the due date for filing a tax return for that year. Extensions to filing a tax return do *not* extend the IRA contribution deadline.

IRA owners may file their tax returns showing one or more IRA contributions before they actually make the contribution. The contribution must, in fact, be made by the due date of the return, usually April 15 of the year following the tax year for which the return is being filed.

---

### ILL. 3.3  *Spousal IRA Contributions*

The following examples illustrate spousal contribution limits:

- Dennis and Jill Cooper file a joint tax return for last year. Jill earned $39,000 and Dennis earned $200 that year. Jill contributed $1,900 to her IRA that same year. After speaking with his financial representative, Dennis decided to be treated as having no compensation. Jill established a spousal IRA for Dennis. However, because Jill had already contributed $1,900 to her own IRA, the most that can be contributed to Dennis' (spousal) IRA is $350 ($2,250 minus $1,900).

- Assume the same set of circumstances except that the contribution to the spousal IRA is $2,000, the limit for any IRA. The most Jill can then contribute to her own IRA for last year is $250 ($2,250 minus $2,000).

---

### Designating the Contribution Year

Individuals who open or contribute to an IRA need to make sure that their custodian or trustee credits the contribution to the correct year. Mistakes are most likely to happen when contributions are made between January 1 and April 15 of every year. During this period, IRA contributions could apply either to the past tax year or to the current one.

Sponsors (custodians, trustees, etc.) are required to report the year for which an IRA owner's contributions apply. Sponsors that fail to do so can be fined $50 for each reporting failure.

When individuals have several IRAs or make a number of small contributions for each tax year rather than a single large contribution, it's easy to make an excess contribution simply by losing track of the number and amount of prior contributions for a given tax year. Therefore, IRA owners need to carefully record their contributions for a given year so such mistakes won't occur.

### Make Contributions Early

IRA owners can wait until after sundown on April 15 to make their IRA contributions for the previous year—but should they? Probably not.

---

### ILL. 3.4  *Compensation When Both Spouses Earn More Than $250*

Ken and Maria are a married couple. They both work and each has set up an IRA. Last year, Maria earned $31,000 and Ken earned $1,900. Maria can contribute up to $2,000 to her IRA. Ken can contribute up to $1,900 to his IRA.

Whether they file a joint return or separate return has no impact on the maximum IRA contribution that each can make for the year.

---

---

**ILL. 3.5** *It Pays to Contribute Early*

**L**et's look at two IRA contributors: Eddie Earlybird makes his contribution at the start of each year to an IRA earning 10 percent. Walter Waitawhile makes his contribution to an IRA, earning the same rate on April 15 of the following year. After the first year, Eddie's IRA will have earned $200 and be worth $2,200, while Walter's IRA has not even been opened.

From then on, Eddie's IRA will always exceed Walter's by the compounded effect of the extra 15½ months' earnings for each year's contribution. After five years, Eddie's IRA will have $1,492 more than Walter's; after ten years, $3,979 more; after 20 years, $14,440 more; and after 30 years, $41,570 more.

After 30 years, Eddie's start-of-the-year IRA, in which he has invested $60,000, will be worth $361,887; Walter's tax-deadline IRA, with $58,000 invested, will be worth $318,317.

Why?

The earlier an individual invests in his or her IRA each year, the faster the IRA account will grow. Following this simple strategy can put the IRA owner thousands of dollars ahead at retirement time.

Of course, it's not always possible for your clients to make their entire IRA contributions in early January when most are saddled with holiday bills. Nevertheless, to make the most of their IRAs, encourage your clients to bunch their contributions close to the start of each year rather than waiting until the April 15 tax deadline of the following year. By investing early, your clients' contributions will be compounding tax-sheltered for an extra 15½ months.

## ■ DEDUCTIBILITY OF IRA CONTRIBUTIONS

The deductibility of IRA contributions has been a subject of confusion ever since 1987, when significant changes affecting IRA deductions were put into effect. Before 1987, any contributions an individual made to an IRA (within the contribution limits) were tax deductible.

If an IRA owner or his or her spouse is covered by an employer's retirement plan at any time during the year, an IRA owner's allowable IRA deduction may be less than his or her allowable contributions. Furthermore, in these cases allowable deductions may be reduced or eliminated, depending on the amount of a taxpayer's adjusted gross income. It is important to remember that deduction limits have no affect whatsoever on contribution limits.

### Are Your Clients Covered?

Every year employers must send their workers the Form W-2 "Wage and Tax Statement" for income-tax reporting purposes. The statement includes a box to indicate whether the employee is covered by the employer's plan for the year. The form should have a mark in the "Pension Plan" box if the employee is, indeed, covered.

If your clients are still not certain whether they are covered by their employers' retirement plans, they should then ask their employers. An employer's human resources or employee benefits department should have this information readily available.

## Employer Plans

With an employer-sponsored retirement plan, an employer sets up a retirement plan for the benefit of its employees and their beneficiaries. For purposes of the IRA deduction rules, an employer retirement plan is considered to be a:

- *Qualified pension plan.* This can be a profit-sharing, stock bonus or money-purchase plan that complies with Internal Revenue Code requirements. (Keogh plans are also included in this definition.)

- *401(k) plan.* This is an arrangement in a profit-sharing or stock bonus plan that allows an eligible employee to choose to take part of his or her compensation from an employer in cash or have the employer pay it into the 401(k) plan.

- *Union plan.* This is a qualified stock bonus, pension or profit-sharing plan created by a collective bargaining agreement between employee representatives and one or more employers.

- *Qualified annuity plan.* This type of plan allows employees to fund their annuities through salary reductions. These contributions are made with pre-tax dollars, thus lowering the employees' current taxable income.

- *Federal, state or local government plan.* This type of plan is established by some political entity or agency for its employees. (Certain state-operated deferred compensation plans, known as Section 457 plans, are *not* included in this definition.)

- *Tax-sheltered annuity plan.* This plan is established for employees of public schools, hospitals and certain other tax-exempt organizations.

- *Simplified employee pension (SEP) plan.* This is a employer-maintained retirement plan that often replaces an existing retirement plan. (SEPs will be discussed in Chapter 5.)

- *501(c)(18) trust.* This is a certain type of tax-exempt trust created before June 25, 1959, that is funded only by employee contributions.

### When Is an Employee "Covered?"

Special rules apply to determine whether your clients are considered to be covered by or actively participating in an employer plan for a given tax year. These rules differ depending on whether the plan is a defined contribution or a defined benefit plan. The rules may also reflect your clients' marital status.

---

**ILL. 3.6  *Who Isn't Covered?***

The following individuals are *not* considered covered by an employer plan:

- Single individuals if they are not "active participants" for any part of the year.
- Married individuals if neither they nor their spouses are covered for any part of the year.
- Married individuals filing separate returns, even if their spouses are covered, if the taxpayer and spouse did not live together at any time during the year.
- Individuals who are not working and who are receiving retirement benefits from a previous employer's plan.
- Members of Armed Forces Reserve units who did not serve more than 90 days during the year and most volunteer firefighters who are not entitled to retirement benefits (projected to exceed $1,800 per year at retirement).

---

### Defined Contribution Plans

A *defined contribution plan* provides a separate account for each person covered under the plan. Ultimately, benefits will depend on amounts contributed or allocated to each account and their corresponding tax-deferred earnings. Types of defined contribution plans include profit-sharing plans, stock bonus plans and money purchase (pension) plans.

An employee is considered to be a participant in a defined contribution plan when his or her employer makes a contribution for the plan year or any forfeiture is allocated to his or her account.

### Defined Benefit Plan

Simply put, a *defined benefit plan* is any plan that is *not* a defined contribution plan. Contributions to a defined benefit plan are based on a calculation of the amount of contributions necessary to provide definite benefits to plan participants.

If your clients meet the minimum age (usually 21) and service requirements (usually one year of service with the employer) to participate in a defined benefit plan for the plan year that ends with their tax years, they will be considered covered under the plan. "Active participant" status will apply even if your client declines to be covered under the plan or did not perform the minimum number of hours of work to accrue a benefit for the year.

Even if a participant is not vested in the amount allocated to his or her defined contribution plan or in the accrued benefit in a defined benefit plan, he or she will still be considered covered under the plan for IRA purposes. For example, let's say that an employee is eligible for coverage under his company's defined benefit plan with a July 1 through June 30 plan year. Then the employee decides to leave the company on December 30, 1995. Because this employee is eligible for coverage under the plan for the year ending June 30, 1996, he is considered covered by the plan for his 1996 tax year.

### *Marital Status Impacts Coverage*

In most cases, an individual is considered covered by an employer retirement plan because his or her spouse is covered by one. The IRS determines whether an individual is covered by an employer plan because of a spouse's coverage based on whether that individual is single or married on the last day of the tax year.

If a participant is married and files his or her income tax jointly, then both spouses would be considered covered by a plan if either spouse is covered. However, if a participant is married but files his or her income taxes using separate returns, then both spouses will be treated as covered if either spouse is covered *and* the spouses lived together at any time during the year.

## ■ CONTRIBUTION DEDUCTION LIMITS

We have already discussed that the deduction individuals can take for contributions made to IRAs will depend on whether they and their spouses are covered for any part of the year by an employer's retirement plan, but an IRA owner's contribution deductions will *also* be affected by how much income he or she has, as well as the status of their particular income tax filing.

If neither the IRA owner nor spouse is covered for any part of the year by an employer retirement plan, the owner or spouse can claim a *full* deduction for the amount contributed to an IRA.

However, if either the IRA owner or spouse is covered by an employer retirement plan, he or she may be entitled to only a *reduced (partial) deduction,* depending on income and filing status. The deduction begins to decrease (phase out) when the individual's modified adjusted gross income exceeds $25,000 for single taxpayers and $40,000 for married taxpayers filing jointly. This is known as the "adjusted gross income limitation."

Adjusted gross income (AGI) generally refers to a taxpayer's gross income from all sources (including investments, retirement benefits, taxable IRA benefits, etc.) after reductions for certain items. IRA contributions are *not* subtracted in calculating AGI.

### Filing Status

Your clients' filing statuses depend primarily on their marital statuses. For IRA purposes, individuals filing singly or as heads of household will share the same modified AGI limit tiers. Taxpayers filing jointly or qualifying widows or widowers will also share the same modified AGI limit tiers. Married taxpayers who file separately will have a different modified AGI limit tier.

An individual's IRA deduction is reduced or phased out entirely depending on filing status and modified AGI:

- If the filing status is *single or head of household,* the IRA deduction is reduced (phased out) if modified AGI is between $25,000 and $35,000. The IRA deduction is eliminated entirely if modified AGI is $35,000 or more.

- If the filing status is *married—joint return or qualifying widow(er),* the IRA deduction is reduced (phased out) if modified AGI is between $40,000 and $50,000. The IRA deduction is eliminated entirely if modified AGI is $50,000 or more.

- If the filing status is *married—filing separately,* the IRA deduction is reduced (phased out) if the modified adjusted gross income is between $0 and $10,000. The IRA deduction is eliminated entirely if the modified AGI is $10,000 or more.

(The modified AGI numbers above are not adjusted annually for inflation and have applied since the Tax Reform Act of 1986 became effective.)

## Figuring a Reduced IRA Deduction

If IRA owners are covered or considered covered by an employer retirement plan and their modified AGIs are within the phaseout ranges for the applicable filing status, the IRA contributions deduction must be reduced.

For married taxpayers who both work and contribute to IRAs, the deduction for each spouse should be calculated separately. Individuals who became divorced or legally separated during the year may not deduct any contributions made to a spousal IRA. After a divorce or legal separation, an individual may deduct only the contributions made to his or her own IRA. The amount of the deduction will be determined based on the modified AGI limitation for single taxpayers.

Here are the steps to follow to figure out the contribution deduction for single taxpayers and heads of households:

*Step 1:* Subtract the taxpayer's modified AGI from $35,000. (Note: If the amount of modified AGI is more than $35,000, assume that none of the contribution is tax deductible.)

*Step 2:* Multiply the difference from the first step by 20 percent to determine the deduction.

Let's look at an example.

Gary, a single taxpayer, had a modified AGI of $28,000 in 1995. He is covered under his employer's qualified retirement plan. Gary wishes to contribute to his IRA only in amounts that can be deducted. Gary's 1995 IRA deduction would be figured as follows:

$$
\begin{array}{rl}
\$\,35{,}000 & \text{Top of AGI phaseout window} \\
-28{,}000 & \text{Gary's 1995 modified AGI} \\
\hline
\$\ \ 7{,}000 & \\
\times\ \ \ \ .20 & \\
\hline
\$\ \ 1{,}400 & \text{Gary's 1995 deductible contribution}
\end{array}
$$

While Gary can contribute $2,000, only $1,400 can be deducted from his income tax.

Here are the steps to follow to figure out the contribution deduction for married, joint filers and qualifying widow(er)s:

*Step 1:* Subtract the taxpayer's modified AGI from $50,000. (Note: If the amount of modified AGI is more than $50,000, assume that none of the contribution is tax deductible.)

*Step 2:* Multiply the difference from the first step by 20 percent (or 22.5 percent if a spousal IRA contribution is also being made).

Let's look at an example.

Susan and Dan Shapiro are a married couple, file their taxes jointly and both work. Their modified AGI for 1995 was $47,000. Dan's 1995 IRA contribution deduction would be figured as follows:

$$\begin{array}{rl} \$\,50,000 & \text{Top of AGI phaseout window} \\ -47,000 & \text{Dan's 1995 modified AGI} \\ \hline \$\ \ 3,000 & \\ \times\quad .20 & \\ \hline \$\quad\ \ 600 & \text{Dan's 1995 deductible contribution} \end{array}$$

(Note: A similar calculation should be made to determine the amount of Susan's IRA deduction.)

Obviously, the amounts correctly calculated in the above examples as well as in "real-world" scenarios will always turn out to be less than $2,000. Although they are somewhat complicated to use, worksheets are provided by the IRS to help taxpayers calculate their IRA contribution deductions.

## Reporting Deductible Contributions

Fortunately, IRA owners don't have to itemize deductions to claim their IRA contribution deductions. However, taxpayers who wish to claim deductions for their IRA contributions must file their federal income taxes using IRS Form 1040 or 1040A (rather than the simpler version, the Form 1040EZ). Forms 1040 and 1040A contain special sections for reporting both regular and spousal deductible IRA contributions as well as contributions to IRAs in conjunction with SEP programs.

## Nondeductible IRA Contributions

Although active participants' deductions for IRA contributions may be reduced or eliminated because of the AGI limitation, they may still make contributions of up to $2,000 ($2,250 for a regular and spousal IRA combined) or 100 percent of compensation, whichever is less.

The difference between total permitted contributions and total deductible contributions, if any, is the "nondeductible contribution."

For instance, take the situation of Ken, who is single and covered by an employer retirement plan. In 1995, his modified AGI was $46,235. Ken made a $2,000 contribution for 1995. Ken could not deduct any of his 1995 contribution because he was covered by his employer's retirement plan *and* his modified AGI was more than

## ILL. 3.7 ■ IRA Deduction Worksheet

**For Single Filers and Heads of Household:**

$35,000

| | | | |
|---|---|---|---|
| minus | $ _____ | Taxpayer's modified AGI |
| equals | $ _____ | |
| times | .20 | |
| equals | $ _____ | IRA contribution deduction |

**For Married, Joint Filers and Qualifying Widow(er)s:**

$50,000

| | | | |
|---|---|---|---|
| minus | $ _____ | Taxpayer's modified AGI |
| equals | $ _____ | |
| times | .20 | (Use .225 as multiplier if spousal contribution is included) |
| equals | $ _____ | IRA contribution deduction |

**For Married, Filing Separately:**

$10,000

| | | | |
|---|---|---|---|
| minus | $ _____ | Taxpayer's modified AGI |
| equals | $ _____ | |
| times | .20 | IRA contribution deduction |
| equals | $ _____ | |

$35,000. He may either treat and report the contribution as a nondeductible contribution or (under certain circumstances) withdraw the contribution.

Although Ken in this example is not entitled to a tax deduction for his contribution, making an IRA contribution is not without an important tax advantage. Assuming Ken's contributions are within the limits, none of the earnings on his nondeductible contributions will be taxed until they are distributed.

Keep in mind that when an individual makes a nondeductible IRA contribution, he or she has a *cost basis* in that contribution. This is the sum that he or she contributed to an IRA minus any distributions of those amounts. When an individual receives distributions attributable to these amounts, such distributions are tax free. Assuming a taxpayer has a basis in an IRA, the IRS requires that withdrawals include both taxable and nontaxable amounts, until all basis is recovered. From that point on, any withdrawals would not include any basis and would therefore be fully taxable.

### Reporting Nondeductible Contributions

Although IRA owners must report their nondeductible contributions, they do not have to specify a contribution as nondeductible until they actually file their tax returns.

To designate contributions as nondeductible, IRA owners must file Form 8606, "Nondeductible IRAs (Contributions, Distributions and Basis)." Form 8606 is generally used by a taxpayer who makes nondeductible contributions to an IRA and also when a taxpayer receives distributions and once made nondeductible contributions to any IRA.

Taxpayers may think it is not necessary to report nondeductible IRA contributions, but when taxpayers fail to report nondeductible contributions, certain consequences occur. First, all of the unreported IRA contributions will be treated as deductible, and when the IRA owner makes withdrawals from his or her IRA, the withdrawn amounts will be taxed unless the taxpayer can prove to the IRS that nondeductible contributions were actually made.

Second, the IRS will impose a $50 penalty on taxpayers who do not file the required Form 8606, unless they can prove that the failure to file was due to a reasonable cause. Overstatement of the amount of nondeductible contributions will result in a $100 penalty for each overstatement, unless the taxpayer can show that the error was due to reasonable cause.

## ■ SUMMARY

As we have seen, annual IRA contributions can be made regardless of whether they are deductible. If the taxpayer or the taxpayer's spouse is not an active participant in an employer retirement plan, the contribution will be fully deductible. If the taxpayer (or spouse) is an active participant in an employer's retirement plan, contribution deductibility, if available, will be based on the taxpayer's annual income.

Although taxpayers may make IRA contributions any time before they file their income taxes (without extensions) for a given tax year, contributing as early in the year as possible will ultimately increase an IRA's value because of additional months of tax-deferred compounding each year.

## ■ CHAPTER 3 QUESTIONS FOR REVIEW

1. Which of the following items would *not* be considered "compensation" for IRA purposes?

   a. Tips
   b. Salary
   c. Commissions from sales
   d. Interest earned on a bank certificate of deposit

2. Eric Armstrong earned $1,000 from his job as a waiter last year. He had no other compensation. What is the maximum IRA contribution that Eric can make to an IRA for that year?

   a. $1,000
   b. $2,000
   c. $2,250
   d. $250

3. Last year Carol and John Majors, a married couple, jointly earned $75,000. Mary is an active participant in her employer's qualified retirement plan. If John, who is self-employed, wishes to contribute to an IRA, that contribution will be

   a. fully deductible.
   b. partially deductible.
   c. nondeductible.
   d. conditionally deductible.

4. Phillip Stone, a single taxpayer, had an AGI of $28,000 last year. He is an active participant in his employer's qualified retirement plan. He wishes to make only the maximum *deductible* contribution for that tax year. How much will Phillip contribute?

   a. $2,800
   b. $2,250
   c. $2,000
   d. $1,400

5. Reporting deductible IRA contributions to the IRS is accomplished by

   a. indicating the contribution on the taxpayer's Form 1040.
   b. filing Form IRA or Form IRA-EZ.
   c. filing Form 8606.
   d. None of the above

6. Reporting nondeductible IRA contributions to the IRS is accomplished by

   a. indicating the contribution on the taxpayer's Form 1040.
   b. filing Form IRA or Form IRA-EZ.
   c. filing Form 8606.
   d. Reporting nondeductible IRA contributions is not required.

# 4

# Rollovers and Transfers

The Internal Revenue Service allows tax-free rollovers or transfers of cash or other assets from one retirement program to another to preserve the special tax-deferred status of retirement accounts. People make rollovers for convenience, to obtain a better return on investments or simply because they are unhappy with the party handling their account and want to switch to a new custodian.

Properly handled, rollovers keep eligible money in tax-deferred status; handled improperly, the IRS rejects the rollover, and the participant faces possible penalties and loss of tax-deferred status.

This chapter examines the various types of rollovers available and then looks at the IRS rules that govern rollovers and transfers.

■ ■ ■ ■ ■

## ■ DIFFERENCES BETWEEN ROLLOVERS AND TRANSFERS

The terms "rollover" and "transfer" are typically used to describe any movement of funds from a qualified plan or an IRA to another IRA investment. There are, however, important differences between a rollover and a transfer.

Your client *rolls over* to an IRA when his or her retirement plan is liquidated and a check is sent by the trustee directly to him or her. This would apply when a lump sum distribution is received from a qualified plan or the money is withdrawn from a previously established IRA.

In a rollover situation, the investor has 60 days to reinvest in another IRA (from the time the money is received) without paying current taxes on the rollover amount. Only one rollover is allowed per year, per IRA. If an individual has five IRA accounts, he or she could roll over each account once a year.

An IRA, however, is *transferred* when the money is sent directly by one financial institution to another, bypassing the owner entirely. There are no legal restrictions on the number of times a transfer can take place in a given year. Some custodians, though, may impose restrictions on how many transfers will be permitted in one year and may even impose fees on each transfer. Therefore, the IRA owner should investigate possible restrictions and costs before transferring IRA funds.

## ■ TYPES OF ROLLOVERS

Rollovers come in two types: (1) IRA to IRA and (2) qualified employee plan to an IRA.

### Rollovers from IRA to IRA

A IRA owner may withdraw, tax free, all or part of the assets from an IRA if he or she reinvests the assets within 60 days in another IRA. Because this is a rollover, the IRA owner cannot deduct the amount that he or she invests in the new IRA.

For example, suppose Carlos has his IRA in a CD at a bank. Because interest rates are down and the stock market is zooming, Carlos wants to invest the money in a common stock mutual fund. He may withdraw the money from the bank in the form of a check and mail the check to arrive at the mutual fund within 60 days of the withdrawal, completing the rollover.

Carlos should confirm the arrival of his funds at the mutual fund company as early as possible so that any problems with the rollover can be identified and corrected before the 60-day rollover window expires.

### *Watch the Calendar*

If an IRA owner keeps the money rolled from an IRA in his or her hands longer than the 60-day limit dictated by the IRS, the money becomes ineligible for rollover treatment and must be declared as income.

As stated before, the IRS permits only *one* rollover per account per year. Losing track of the last rollover from a particular IRA account can cause potential problems with the IRS.

Consider this scenario: On April 20, Wanda, who is 40 years old, requests that Lincoln Bank, at which she has an IRA invested in a CD, send her a check for the account when the CD expires. On May 1, Wanda receives a check for $2,500. Wanda spends the money on a vacation, then notices that the First National Bank is offering a 9 percent rate on three-month CDs. Wanda borrows another $2,500 from her sister and starts a CD at First National Bank, telling First National that this is a rollover from Lincoln Bank. Wanda closes the deal June 28, beating the 60-day deadline. She claims this as a rollover. So far, the IRS agrees.

In mid–July, Wanda requests and receives $5,000 from another IRA account at First National. Immediately, she puts the money into an IRA mutual fund account, claiming it as a rollover. On September 28, that three-month CD at First National Bank matures (the one established on June 28). Wanda picks up a check for $2,500 plus $56.25 interest from First National. She consolidates the money with the $5,000 mutual fund account, claiming this as a rollover. This time the IRS does *not* agree.

Why?

Wanda already rolled over that $2,500 only a few months earlier from Lincoln to First National. Wanda owes current income taxes on the $2,556.25. She also faces a 10 percent penalty because she is under age 59½.

Wanda's problem might have been avoided had she directly transferred her funds on an institution-to-institution basis. If the bank had transferred the money directly to the mutual fund at Wanda's request, she would technically have made a transfer, not a rollover, with its limit of one permitted per account per year. With a transfer her money would go to her destination just the same, and Wanda doesn't risk breaking the rollover rule.

### Inherited IRAs

If an individual inherits an IRA or qualified plan funds from his or her deceased spouse, he or she can generally roll it over into an IRA. If an individual inherits an IRA from someone other than a spouse, he or she can neither roll it over nor allow it to be received as a rollover contribution.

## ■ ROLLOVERS FROM QUALIFIED PLANS

Thanks to the availability of IRA rollovers, it's possible to postpone the taxation of qualified plan benefits at the time of distribution. This is accomplished by rolling over within 60 days the plan distribution, totally or in part, into an IRA or into another qualified pension or profit-sharing plan. The earnings will then continue to accumulate tax deferred until withdrawals are made.

A *partial rollover* occurs when an employee receives a distribution from a qualified plan and then decides to roll over only a portion of the distribution. The portion retained, of course, must be reported as income; the portion rolled over will remain tax deferred.

Under prior laws, your clients had to roll over at least 50 percent of their distributions in order to continue tax deferral. Since January 1993, a participant can retain any portion of a distribution and then transfer the remaining amount into an IRA rollover or another employer's qualified retirement plan.

### Withholding Tax on Qualified Plan Rollovers

Since January 1, 1993, employers have to withhold 20 percent of distributions from a qualified plan unless the employee tells the employer to transfer directly or roll over this amount to an IRA or other qualified plan. This 20 percent withholding rule applies even if the participant completes the rollover within the required 60 days. Note, however, that the full amount of the distribution, including the 20 percent withheld, must be rolled over if the employee wants to avoid all taxes and penalties. This is explained in Ill. 4.1.

A direct rollover may be made by a wire transfer or check mailed to the IRA or a new employer's qualified retirement plan. The IRS is mainly concerned that the check is payable or is transferred directly to the trustee or custodian. It is acceptable

---

**ILL. 4.1  *20 Percent Withholding—A Case Study***

**C**onsider the following situation when it comes to the 20 percent withholding requirement:

Peter Connors, age 53, is director of communications for a manufacturing firm. Peter is in the 28 percent marginal income tax bracket. He is to receive $100,000 from his employer's qualified plan. Because he chooses to receive a direct cash distribution personally, he will receive only $80,000. To make the distribution entirely tax free, Peter would have to put an amount equal to the entire distribution—$100,000—into another qualified plan or an IRA. If the missing $20,000 is not included in the rollover amount, it will be treated as taxable.

This means that Peter must roll over the $80,000 and make up the missing $20,000 from his own pocket. Assuming Peter does not have an extra $20,000 available, he will owe income taxes on the withheld $20,000 (20 percent of the total distribution) plus a 10 percent penalty (because he is under 59½). Based on Peter's 28 percent marginal income tax bracket, he will owe $5,600 in regular income tax *plus* an additional $2,000 in early withdrawal penalties, for a combined tax liability of $7,600.

The IRS will return the withheld funds after the employee files a tax return, as long as the full distribution is rolled over within 60 days into another employee plan or IRA. Because the withheld 20 percent is treated as a taxable distribution, the employee will need to make up the withheld 20 percent from his or her own funds to accomplish a 100 percent tax-free rollover. Otherwise, the 20 percent will be treated as taxable. Aside from the income taxes owed on the amount, the employee will also pay a 10 percent penalty if he or she is under age 59½.

---

to provide the departing employee with a check payable to the trustee of the eligible plan.

The plan making the direct distribution must comply with this requirement. Employees who do not directly rollover and receive distributions themselves will receive only 80 percent of their account because 20 percent will be withheld.

### Avoiding the Withholding Tax

To avoid the withholding tax, the participant should request a direct trustee-to-trustee transfer to a new qualified plan or IRA. A direct transfer is the only way to escape the 20 percent withholding requirement. Qualified plans must permit employees who request rollover distributions to elect a direct trustee-to-trustee transfer.

However, if the intent is to roll the funds over to another qualified plan, there is a possibility that the new plan will not accept such transfers. Before a participant makes his or her direct transfer plans, he or she should confirm that the new (transferee) plan will accept the funds directly. Indeed, because of potential recordkeeping problems, many qualified plans won't accept funds from other plans.

The administrator of an employer's qualified plan must provide employees who request a distribution a written explanation (within a reasonable period of time) that must, at a minimum, contain the following information:

- the taxpayer's right to have the distribution paid tax free directly to an IRA or other eligible retirement plan;

- the employer's requirement to withhold tax from the distribution if it is not paid directly to an IRA or other eligible retirement plan;

- the nontaxability of any part of the distribution that is rolled over into an IRA or another eligible retirement plan within 60 days from receipt of the distribution; and

- if applicable, other rules pertaining to the employer's qualified plan, including those for lump-sum distributions, alternate payees in divorce situations and cash or deferred arrangements.

The IRS defines a "reasonable period of time" as "no earlier than 90 days and no later than 30 days before the distribution is made."

Under certain circumstances a participant may need to receive a distribution in less than 30 days after the explanation has been provided. The IRS will allow such distributions as long as both of the following two requirements are met:

- The employee must have the opportunity to consider whether he or she wants to make a direct rollover for at least 30 days after the explanation is provided.

- The information sent to the taxpayer must clearly state that he or she has 30 days to make a decision between receiving funds or arranging for a direct rollover.

Plan participants, that is, employees, must also cooperate in the process by providing the plan administrator with timely information about the other qualified plan or IRA to which the transfer will be made.

## ■ ELIGIBLE ROLLOVER DISTRIBUTIONS

Only eligible distributions from a taxpayer's (or the taxpayer's deceased spouse) qualified plan may be rolled over entirely or partially into an IRA. The distribution must come from an employer's pension, profit-sharing plan, stock bonus plan, annuity plan or tax-sheltered annuity plan (403(b) plan) that meets the Internal Revenue Code requirements for qualified plans.

An eligible rollover distribution is usually the taxable part of any distribution from a qualified retirement plan, except for a required minimum distribution and any of a series of substantially equal periodic distributions paid at least once a year over (1) the taxpayer's lifetime or life expectancy, (2) the lifetimes or life expectancies of the taxpayer and his or her beneficiary, or (3) a period of 10 years or more.

### Insurance Contracts

When a participant's qualified plan contains life insurance contracts, transferring into an IRA is probably a poor choice. Although property other than cash may be rolled into an IRA, the Internal Revenue Code specifically disallows the investment of IRA funds in life insurance.

---

### ILL. 4.2  *Making Choices*

If an individual has a choice between keeping retirement funds in a company pension plan or in an IRA, he or she is almost always better off choosing the IRA. The IRA provides more flexibility than most company plans. Here are some reasons why:

- *Distributions.* Many company plans offer the participant annuity distributions on a fixed schedule. An IRA gives the participant many more alternatives. Of course, the participant may acquire an annuity contract within the framework of the IRA and thus take the same type of annuity payout (from the IRA) that would generally be available from the typical employer retirement plan.

  However, the participant may be more concerned with continuing to defer taxes than receiving a life income. With an IRA, an individual may take only minimum distributions to keep as much money as possible in the IRA for as long as possible to let tax-deferred investment returns keep growing.

- *Investments.* An IRA lets the participant make almost any type of investment that he or she would like. Because funds left in employer-qualified plans are controlled by the plan trustee, the employee may have limited control over how the funds are investe, or worse, he or she may have no control at all.

- *Withdrawals.* IRA owners can withdraw their money early, even if it means paying a penalty. The decision belongs to them. Qualified plans are much more stringent.

- *Beneficiaries.* Employees are legally required to name their spouses as the beneficiaries of their companies' qualified retirement plans, unless the spouse agrees, in writing, to a different beneficiary.

  However, with an IRA, the participant can name a child or grandchild as the beneficiary so that the child can inherit the account. (The IRA must still be maintained in the deceased IRA owner's name for the benefit of the child.)

- *Security.* Unfortunately, many of today's company pension plans are underfunded. Even if employers and their qualified plans are healthy now, it's risky to assume that such plans will not falter years from now when participants must depend on them for retirement income. With an IRA, participants know that the money is available. It remains under the participant's control.

---

An employee may not transfer a distributed life insurance contract into an IRA. Moreover, the value of the life insurance contract, except for amounts that were considered to have been distributed to the employee, are immediately taxable to the employee.

### Keogh to IRA Rollovers

Participants who are self-employed are generally treated as "employees" for rollover purposes. Participants may roll over part or all of a distribution from a Keogh plan into an IRA or other eligible retirement plan.

If the recipient of a distribution from a Keogh plan is under 59½, self-employed and not disabled, any payout from an operating Keogh cannot be treated as a lump-sum distribution, meaning it will not qualify for forward-averaging tax treatment. Thus, a rollover might be an attractive alternative.

### Rollovers from Tax-Sheltered Annuities

An eligible distribution from a tax-sheltered annuity (TSA) plan can be rolled over into an IRA or into another tax-sheltered annuity plan.

A TSA is a retirement vehicle to meet the needs of employees of certain nonprofit, charitable, education and religious organizations. Contributions to a TSA are excluded from a participant's gross income, and his or her earnings in a TSA accumulate tax free until distributed.

However, a TSA cannot be rolled into another type of retirement plan, such as a qualified pension plan.

### Conduit IRAs

When an individual transfers money from a qualified plan and anticipates that he or she might later want to roll those funds into another qualified plan, he or she should set up a *new* IRA to hold the rollover funds rather than mixing them with a previously established IRA. In fact, a participant should establish a new and completely separate rollover account every time he or she leaves a company taking a retirement plan distribution.

Keeping the IRA rollover separate from other IRAs preserves a participant's right to roll that account later into a new employer's plan if the new employer will accept the rollover. An IRA established to receive qualified plan rollovers is generally known as a *conduit IRA*.

Conduit IRAs can be viewed as a temporary holding place for distributions that are received from qualified plans. The purpose of a conduit IRA is to allow the participant to put distributions from qualified plans into a temporary—and tax-sheltered—place until the distributions can be rolled over into another plan.

### ■ SUMMARY

Rollovers and transfers of a participant's individual and employer-sponsored retirement accounts are permitted by the IRS so that retirement accounts can still maintain their tax-deferred status.

Rollovers involve a distribution to the account owner while transfers are made payable to the custodian/trustee of a successor IRA or qualified retirement plan. Only one rollover is allowed per year, per IRA account.

Many nondirect distributions from qualified plans are subject to special 20 percent withholding requirements. The 20 percent withholding requirement may be avoided by arranging for a direct transfer between trustees and custodians.

## ■ CHAPTER 4 QUESTIONS FOR REVIEW

1. A rollover

   a. is subject to the $2,000 annual contribution limit.
   b. is exactly the same as a transfer.
   c. is a tax-free distribution of assets from one retirement program to another.
   d. is permissible only from one IRA account into another IRA account.

2. All the statements below regarding rollovers are true EXCEPT

   a. A taxpayer is permitted one rollover per IRA account, per year.
   b. A taxpayer has 60 days in which to complete a rollover.
   c. A rollover is generally made payable to a successor custodian or trustee.
   d. A rollover generally involves a distribution that is payable to the account owner.

3. Which of the following techniques will help a participant avoid the 20 percent withholding associated with distributions from qualified retirement plans?

   a. Keeping transfers under $2,000 per year
   b. Arranging for a direct trustee-to-trustee transfer
   c. Signing a withholding waiver
   d. Any of the above

4. In most circumstances, qualified plan assets may NOT be rolled into an IRA if the qualified plan contains

   a. life insurance.
   b. mutual funds.
   c. cash.
   d. bonds.

5. When a taxpayer moves assets from a qualified plan into an IRA, he or she should generally

   a. combine the funds with existing IRAs.
   b. establish a separate IRA to receive the rollover or transfer.
   c. establish a new qualified plan to receive the rollover.
   d. None of the above

6. An IRA that is a temporary holding place for distributions received from a qualified plan is generally known as a

   a. holding IRA.
   b. temporary IRA.
   c. conduit IRA.
   d. partial IRA.

# 5

# Simplified Employee Pensions

**S** *implified employee pensions* (SEPs) are a relatively easy tax-saving and retirement device that can be used by self-employed individuals as well as businesses. SEPs were created under the Revenue Act of 1978. The purpose behind SEPs was to help smaller businesses provide retirement benefits for employees without as much of the red tape and administrative burden associated with regular employer pension plans.

A SEP is like an oversized IRA, allowing the contributor to save much more every year than the regular IRA limit of $2,000. Despite its many similarities to regular IRAs, SEPs operate under different rules.

Many people and businesses are eligible to start SEPs but don't know it. (Partnerships and corporations may also establish SEPs.) Compared to other types of business-sponsored retirement plans, SEPs are easy to administer and have low start-up costs. This chapter explains the structure of SEPs and how the financial representative can communicate a SEP's advantages to business owners and self-employed individuals.

■ ■ ■ ■ ■

## ■ STRUCTURE OF SEPs

Employer contributions to SEPs are excluded from an employee's gross income and are not subject to employment taxes. In certain SEP programs, employees may also make voluntary contributions through salary reductions or other types of optional elective deferrals.

A SEP is a remarkably flexible plan because employer contributions are not required every year. Contributions may vary from year to year, provided that each person covered by the plan receives the same percentage of income as a contribution.

A SEP may also be integrated with Social Security, a feature that may allow a higher percentage of compensation to be contributed for higher-paid employees. The only other type of business retirement plan that offers this degree of flexibility is a profit-sharing plan that carries far more stringent administrative and reporting responsibilities than those required with a SEP program.

## SEP Contributions

Under a SEP plan, *contributions* are made by an employer (and in certain cases, which will be discussed later, by an employee) to individual retirement arrangements, known as *SEP-IRAs,* for all qualified employees.

A SEP-IRA for a given tax year may be established and funded no later than the due date—plus extensions—of a business' or self-employed individual's income tax return for that year. It may be established as early as the first day of the calendar year for which the first contributions are made. In most cases, only cash contributions may be made to a SEP-IRA, except in rollover situations.

As mentioned earlier, the employer (remember that for SEPs, a self-employed individual is both employer *and* employee) is not required to make contributions every year, but any contributions must be based on a written allocation formula that does not discriminate in favor of highly compensated employees.

For example, unless the plan is integrated with Social Security, if the employer gives a $100,000-a-year employee a $10,000 contribution, which represents 10 percent of income, a $30,000 employee must receive a $3,000 contribution.

A *highly compensated employee* is an individual who, during the current or preceding tax year:

- owned more than 5 percent of the capital or interest in the profits of the business providing the SEP;

- received annual compensation from the business of more than $100,000 (for 1996);

- received compensation from the business of more than $66,000 (for 1996) and was among the top 20 percent of the highest paid employees during the year; or

- was an officer of the business at any time during the tax year and received annual compensation of more than $60,000 (for 1996).

Assuming contributions will be made for a particular tax year, generally contributions must be made for all qualifying employees who:

- are over age 21;

- worked for the business in at least three of the immediately preceding five years; and

---

### ILL. 5.1  *SEPs and the Entrepreneur*

SEPs are especially attractive for independent entrepreneurs who work alone. Take this example: Barbara Silvers runs a one-person computer training business from her home. In 1995, her compensation from the business was $50,000.

If Barbara maintains only a garden-variety IRA, the most she can contribute and potentially deduct for 1995 is $2,000. If Barbara starts a Keogh plan, a type of retirement plan for the self-employed, she may make contributions that are larger than the $2,000 limit for an IRA, but Barbara may also face recordkeeping and reporting requirements—and recordkeeping is Barbara's least favorite task of entrepreneurship.

A SEP is a great retirement plan choice for Barbara. With a SEP plan, Barbara can make higher contributions (up to 13.0435 percent of her earnings from the business), or $6,521, which is far greater than a regular IRA's annual $2,000 contribution limit.

Better still, Barbara avoids the recordkeeping that may be required with a Keogh plan. A SEP allows Barbara to adjust her annual contributions (within the limits) to correspond with the years when her cashflow needs overshadow her need for retirement savings and income-tax deductions.

---

- received at least $400 (for 1996) from the business. (This amount is indexed annually for inflation.)

An employer must contribute for all employees who meet these *participation requirements* during the year, even though one or more of the employees is no longer employed on the contribution date. Union employees whose retirement benefits were determined by good faith bargaining and certain nonresident aliens don't have to be covered under a SEP.

Assuming that a SEP plan is not discriminatory, the employer may deduct from its taxes any contributions to employees' SEP-IRA accounts

### Contribution Limits

For tax years beginning after 1993, annual contributions made by a business to an employee's SEP-IRA may not exceed 15 percent of the first $150,000 of gross compensation, or $22,500. The IRS defines compensation for SEP purposes in much the same way as it does for regular IRAs.

Self-employed individuals are subject to somewhat more restrictive special rules. They must limit contributions to 15 percent of net earnings from self-employment. (*Net earnings* can be defined as net profits minus one-half self-employment tax [Schedule SE] minus the owner's contributions for self.)

### Figuring Owner/Employee Contributions

Figuring the contribution for the owner/employee of a business sponsoring a SEP plan can be complicated. Fortunately, the IRS provides a "Self-Employed Person's Rate Table" that can be helpful. (See Ill. 5.2.)

### ILL. 5.2 ■ Self-Employed Person's Rate Table

| If the plan contribution rate is: (shown as a percentage) | The self-employed person's rate is: (shown as a decimal) |
|:---:|:---:|
| 1 | .009901 |
| 2 | .019608 |
| 3 | .029126 |
| 4 | .038462 |
| 5 | .047619 |
| 6 | .056604 |
| 7 | .065421 |
| 8 | .074074 |
| 9 | .082569 |
| 10 | .090909 |
| 11 | .099099 |
| 12 | .107143 |
| 13 | .115044 |
| 14 | .122807 |
| 15 | .130435 |

(Source: IRS Publication 560)

Let's take the example of a small business that will contribute 12 percent for "common-law" employees—those who perform services for, and are directed by, the employer.

Assume the owner has net earnings of $100,000 after subtracting one-half self-employment tax from gross earnings. "Gross" earnings will be determined by the amount the business owner reports on the appropriate unincorporated business tax schedule. (Examples include Schedule C for unincorporated businesses, Schedule F for farmers and ranchers and Schedule K for partnerships.)

The "Self-Employed Person's Rate Table" reveals what percentage may be contributed for the owner/employee. The table shows that at a 12 percent contribution level for employees, the owner/employee may contribute 10.7143 percent, or $10,714.

If contributions for employees are not made in whole percentages, the Self-Employed Person's Rate Table is inappropriate for figuring the owner/employee's annual contribution. In such cases, the Self-Employed Person's SEP Deduction Worksheet would be a better tool. (See Ill. 5.3.)

### *Treatment of Excess Contributions*

If the annual amount contributed to an employee's SEP-IRA is more than 15 percent of the first $150,000 of compensation (or more than the amount allowed for the owner), any contribution in excess of the limit will generally be subject to a 6 percent excise tax unless it is withdrawn by the date the applicable income tax return is due (including extensions). In most instances, an excess contribution to a SEP-IRA is treated as a contribution by the employee to his or her own regular IRA.

---

### ILL. 5.3 ■ Self-Employed Person's SEP Deduction Worksheet

1. Contribution rate in plan shown as a decimal  _____

2. Rate in Step 1 plus one  _____

3. Reduced rate for self-employed person (divide Step 1 by Step 2)  _____

4. Net earnings from self-employment  $_____

5. Deduction for self-employment tax
   (one-half self-employment tax—Schedule SE)  $_____

6. Subtract Step 5 from Step 4  $_____

7. Multiply Step 6 by Step 3  $_____

8. Multiply $150,000 by contribution rate in Step 1  $_____

9. Enter *smaller* of Step 7 or Step 8. This is the maximum
   SEP contribution  $_____

---

### Salary Reduction SEPs (SARSEPs)

A SEP can also include a *salary reduction arrangement*. Under this arrangement, employees may choose to have their employers contribute part of their pay to their SEP-IRAs. This choice is called an "elective deferral" because the amount contributed is deferred and the choice regarding whether to contribute rests with the employee.

IRS Form 5305A-SEP may be used to establish this type of SEP, which is often called a SARSEP. Many financial institutions provide model documents to complete the salary reduction SEP-IRA paperwork.

Certain special restrictions apply to salary reduction SEPs. The salary reduction arrangement is available only if:

- at least 50 percent of the employees eligible to participate in the salary reduction arrangement actually elect to do so;

- the business has no more than 25 employees who were eligible to participate in the SEP (or would have been eligible to participate in a SEP had it been previously established) at any time during the preceding year; and

- the annual deferral percentage by each highly compensated employee (as defined earlier) is no more than 125 percent of the average deferral percentage (ADP) of all eligible nonhighly compensated employees.* State or local governments and their subdivisions (that maintain SEP programs), as well as other tax-exempt organizations, may not implement salary reduction arrangements.

---

*This required standard to eliminate discrimination is called the *ADP test*. To illustrate how the ADP test works, let's assume that the lower-paid employee defers an average of 8 percent under the SEP plan. Thus, the highly paid could defer no more than 10 percent on average ($8 \times 1.25 = 10$ percent) of their salary.

---

### ILL. 5.4 ■ SEP Contribution Worksheet Example

Tom McGraw operates an apparel store as a sole proprietor. He has three employees who collectively earned $60,000 in 1995. The terms of the SEP plan that he established provide that as the self-employed principal, Tom contributes 15 percent of net earnings for himself and 15 percent of gross pay for his employees.

Tom's net earnings from the business (not taking into account deductions for self-employment tax or contributions to Tom's own SEP-IRA) are $105,000. In figuring this amount, Tom deducted his employees' pay of $60,000 and contributions for them of 15 percent of pay, or $9,000.

The worksheet below calculates Tom's maximum contribution for his SEP-IRA.

| | |
|---|---:|
| 1. Contribution rate in plan shown as a decimal | .15 |
| 2. Rate in Step 1 plus one | 1.15 |
| 3. Reduced rate for self-employed person (divide Step 1 by Step 2) | .130435 |
| 4. Net earnings from self-employment | $105,000 |
| 5. Deduction for self-employment tax | $ 5,163 |
| 6. Subtract Step 5 from Step 4 | $ 99,837 |
| 7. Multiply Step 6 by Step 3 | $ 13,022 |
| 8. Multiply $150,000 by contribution rate in Step 1 | $ 22,500 |
| 9. Enter *smaller* of Step 7 or Step 8 | $ 13,022 |

The most Tom can contribute to his SEP-IRA is $13,022. He can also deduct this amount from his income for tax purposes.

(Note: The rates in the table and worksheets shown above apply only to unincorporated employers who have only one defined contribution retirement plan.)

## Elective Deferral Limitations

The largest compensation an individual may elect to defer in a single tax year is the smaller of 15 percent of the participant's compensation (defined for an employee as his or her pay from the employer) or $9,500 (for 1996). An employee may also participate in a *403(b) tax-sheltered annuity* (discussed in Chapter 4), which is generally a salary reduction-based retirement program for employees of public school systems and certain nonprofit organizations. In such cases, total elective deferrals relating to both plans may not exceed $9,500.

With a SARSEP, annual funding comes from two sources: the business through its contribution and the employee from voluntary salary reduction. Nevertheless, the *overall* limits (e.g., 15 percent of the first $150,000 of an employee's compensation or 13.0435 percent of an owner/employer's compensation) on contributions apply just as if the SEP plan had no salary reduction feature.

## Tax Treatment of Deferrals

Assuming deferrals do not exceed the limits mandated by the ADP test, they are not included as part of the employee's compensation and therefore, are not subject to federal income tax in the year of the deferral.

## ILL. 5.5 ■ Employee Income Tax Deduction for SEP

| Adjustments to Income | | | | | | | |
|---|---|---|---|---|---|---|---|
| **Adjustments to Income**  Caution: See instructions .... ▶ | 23a | Your IRA deduction (see page 19) ...................... | 23a | | | | |
| | b | Spouse's IRA deduction (see page 19) ................. | 23b | | | | |
| | 24 | Moving expenses. Attach Form 3903 or 3903-F .......... | 24 | | | | |
| | 25 | One-half of self-employment tax ...................... | 25 | | | | |
| | 26 | Self-employed health insurance deduction (see page 21) ... | 26 | | | | |
| | 27 | Keogh retirement plan and self-employed SEP deduction ... | 27 | | | | |
| | 28 | Penalty on early withdrawal of savings................. | 28 | | | | |
| | 29 | Alimony paid. Recipient's SSN ▶ _____ | 29 | | | | |
| | 30 | Add lines 23a through 29. These are your total adjustments ......................... ▶ | 30 | | | | |

However, elective deferral amounts *are* subject to Social Security (FICA) taxation, Medicare tax and federal unemployment tax (FUTA). Thus, contributions relating to elective deferrals under SARSEPs will appear on the employee's (wage) Form W-2, but not in terms of federal income tax liability.

For example, Kathy Wilcox, an employee of Technojet Co. has an annual salary of $30,000. Under a salary reduction arrangement, she chooses to reduce her wages by $4,500 and have that amount contributed by Technojet to a SEP-IRA.

On Kathy's Form W-2, Technojet will report total wages of $25,500 ($30,000 minus $4,500), Social Security wages of $30,000 and Medicare wages of $30,000. Kathy will report $25,500 on her personal income-tax return (Form 1040).

## ■ PROHIBITED TRANSACTIONS

If an account owner (also known as a "party in interest") uses a SEP-IRA improperly, the IRS will say that the party has engaged in a *prohibited transaction.* In such a case, the SEP-IRA will no longer qualify as an IRA.

If a SEP-IRA is disqualified because of a prohibited transaction involving the account owner (rather than the employer offering the SEP program), the assets in the account will be treated as having been distributed to the owner on the first day of the year in which the transaction took place. The owner must then report as income the excess of the asset's fair market value over his or her cost basis in the account. The owner may also face premature distribution penalties if he or she is younger than 59½.

Prohibited transactions on the part of a SEP account owner can cause problems with respect to his or her own individual account but will not affect the employer's overall SEP program.

Certain transactions between the plan and a "disqualified person" are prohibited. An excise tax is charged on such transactions, and the disqualified person who engages in the prohibited transaction is generally liable for the excise tax. If more than one disqualified person takes part in the transaction, each person can be jointly and severally liable for the tax.

A *disqualified person* is considered to be an individual or entity that:

- employs participants in the SEP plan;

- is a 10 percent or more partner in a partnership having the plan;

- is a fiduciary of the plan;

- is a highly compensated employee (measured as one who receives 10 percent or more of the employer's yearly wages);

- is an employee organization having members who are covered by the plan; or

- provides services to the plan.

The IRS also lists certain "related disqualified persons" who also fall under the prohibited transaction rules. *Related disqualified persons* are:

- members of a disqualified person's family (family members are defined as spouses, ancestors, and direct descendants as well as any spouse of a direct descendant); or

- corporations, partnerships, trusts, or estates that own, either directly or indirectly, at least half of:

    a. the total voting stock or the value of all the stock of the corporation offering a SEP;

    b. the capital interest or profit interest in a partnership offering a SEP; or

    c. a beneficial interest in the trust or estate.

The Internal Revenue Code specifies which transactions by a disqualified person (or a related disqualified person) are prohibited. The common thread that links the various prohibited transactions together is whether a real or perceived conflict of interest exists between the disqualified person and the SEP plan.

Distributions of benefits in which disqualified persons would normally be entitled under the SEP-IRA arrangement are, of course, not regarded as prohibited transactions. However, such benefits must conform with nondiscrimination practices.

Prohibited transactions include:

- a transfer of SEP income or assets or income to, or use of them by or for the benefit of, a disqualified person;

- any handling of SEP income or assets by a fiduciary in his or her own interests;

- the receipt of consideration (money or other items of value) by a SEP fiduciary for his or her own account from a party who is dealing with the SEP program in a transaction involving the SEP program's income or assets; and

- acts between the SEP plan and disqualified persons involving the selling, exchanging or leasing of property; lending money or extending credit; and furnishing goods, services or facilities.

In addition, a loan from a SEP-IRA to an owner/employee is also a prohibited transaction.

### Tax on Prohibited Transactions

The tax on a prohibited transaction is 5 percent of the amount involved in the prohibited transaction for each full or partial tax year. Form 5330 must accompany payment of the tax.

If the disallowed transaction is not corrected within the taxable period (which starts on the transaction date and ends the earliest of when the prohibited transaction is corrected or the IRS mails a notice of deficiency or assesses the penalty tax), an additional tax of 100 percent of the amount involved is imposed. (A 90-day extension on the taxable period may be available under certain complex circumstances.)

Correcting a prohibited transaction involves "undoing" it to the extent that the SEP program is not placed in a worse financial position by the correction.

The amount involved in a prohibited transaction is the greater of the money and fair market value of any property given or the money and fair market value of any property received. If actual services are performed by a disqualified person, the amount involved is any excess over reasonable compensation for providing such services.

## ■ REPORTING AND DISCLOSURE REQUIREMENTS

Simplicity of reporting and disclosure is a significant advantage of SEPs relative to other types of retirement plans that may be offered by businesses. Employers can use *Form 5305-SEP,* shown at the end of this chapter, to establish their plans. This form is to be signed by both the employer and the employee (if the employee is a separate individual). Form *5305A-SEP* should be used to set up a SARSEP.

The employer must file "simplified employer reports" with respect to employer contributions. In addition, the employer must report annual contributions for each employee subject to a $10 penalty per required report for failure to do so.

An employer using standard IRS forms to set up the SEP plan can satisfy the reporting and disclosure requirements by giving each employee a copy of the completed agreement form (including its questions and answers) and a statement each year showing any contributions to the employee's SEP-IRA. Employers who maintain salary reduction SEPs must also provide a notice indicating any excess contributions.

An employer who has not used standard IRS Form 5305-SEP or Form 5305A-SEP must provide employees with general SEP information and otherwise satisfy the reporting and disclosure requirements of the Internal Revenue Code. An employer setting up a SEP-IRA plan is required to give employees a disclosure statement that includes a description of the SEP, requirements concerning employer payments and information on the tax status of the employer's contribution as well as questions and answers about the SEP.

The IRS says that if an employer "selects, recommends or substantially influences" employees' IRA investment choices, then the employer must provide a "clearly written explanation" of the features of such choices. Ultimately, the choice of where to set up an IRA must always rest with the employee, no matter what other arrangement the employer may have in mind.

## ■ SUMMARY

The SEP program was specifically designed for self-employed individuals and small businesses. SEPs are intended to operate either as an alternative to the usual qualified pension and profit-sharing plan or as a supplement to a qualified plan.

Employers who establish and maintain SEP programs may not discriminate in favor of highly paid employees and must, assuming contributions are made in a given tax year, contribute for employees who meet the participation requirements. However, the employer is not required to make contributions every year. When contributions are made, they are limited to 15 percent of the first $150,000 of an employee's gross compensation. For owner/employees, the contribution limit is 13.0435 percent of compensation. Employers may deduct contributions made to employees' SEP accounts.

Although reporting and disclosure requirements are far less stringent under a SEP arrangement than they are for other qualified plans, annual employer contributions must be reported to the IRS as well as to applicable employees. Both employers and employees are prohibited from engaging in certain transactions that involve conflicts of interest.

The rules and regulations that govern IRA distributions also apply to SEPs. In the next chapter, we'll focus on distributions and how they relate to your clients' IRAs or SEPs.

## ■ CHAPTER 5 QUESTIONS FOR REVIEW

1. Which of the following types of entities may establish a SEP plan?

   a. Sole proprietors
   b. Partnerships
   c. Corporations
   d. All of the above

2. For SEP purposes, a self-employed individual is regarded as an

   a. employer.
   b. employee.
   c. Both a and b
   d. Neither a nor b

3. All of the statements below regarding SEPs are correct EXCEPT

   a. The employer must commit to making contributions each year.
   b. Contributions may vary from year to year provided that each employee receives the same percentage contribution.
   c. Contributions must be made based on a written allocation formula.
   d. The employer must contribute for all employees who meet the participation requirements during the year.

4. SEP contributions must be made for all employees who

   a. are age 21 or older.
   b. have worked for the employer for at least three out of the past five years.
   c. have earned at least $400 from the employer (for 1996).
   d. All of the above

5. What is the maximum annual dollar contribution that can be made to a nonowner employee's SEP-IRA?

   a. $2,000
   b. $15,000
   c. $22,500
   d. $30,000

6. What is the maximum percentage contribution that may be made to the SEP account of an owner/employee?

   a. 13.0435 percent
   b. 15 percent
   c. 25 percent
   d. 30 percent

7. Which of the following activities represents a prohibited transaction in conjunction with a SEP plan?

   a. A transfer of income or assets from a SEP plan for the benefit of a disqualified person
   b. Selling or leasing property to a SEP program by a disqualified person
   c. Both a and b
   d. Neither a nor b

**Form 5305**
(Rev. October 1992)
Department of the Treasury
Internal Revenue Service

## Individual Retirement Trust Account
(Under Section 408(a) of the Internal Revenue Code)

DO NOT File
with the Internal
Revenue Service

| Name of grantor | Date of birth of grantor | Identifying number (see instructions) |
|---|---|---|
| Address of grantor | | |
| | | Check if Amendment. ▶ ☐ |
| Name of trustee | Address or principal place of business of trustee | |

The Grantor whose name appears above is establishing an individual retirement account under section 408(a) to provide for his or her retirement and for the support of his or her beneficiaries after death.

The Trustee named above has given the Grantor the disclosure statement required under Regulations section 1.408-6.

The Grantor has assigned the trust_____ dollars ($_____) in cash.

The Grantor and the Trustee make the following agreement:

### Article I

The Trustee may accept additional cash contributions on behalf of the Grantor for a tax year of the Grantor. The total cash contributions are limited to $2,000 for the tax year unless the contribution is a rollover contribution described in section 402(c) (but only after December 31, 1992), 403(a)(4), 403(b)(8), 408(d)(3), or an employer contribution to a simplified employee pension plan as described in section 408(k). Rollover contributions before January 1, 1993, include rollovers described in section 402(a)(5), 402(a)(6), 402(a)(7), 403(a)(4), 403(b)(8), 408(d)(3), or an employer contribution to a simplified employee pension plan described in section 408(k).

### Article II

The Grantor's interest in the balance in the trust account is nonforfeitable.

### Article III

1. No part of the trust funds may be invested in life insurance contracts, nor may the assets of the trust account be commingled with other property except in a common trust fund or common investment fund (within the meaning of section 408(a)(5)).

2. No part of the trust funds may be invested in collectibles (within the meaning of section 408(m)) except as otherwise permitted by section 408(m)(3) which provides an exception for certain gold and silver coins and coins issued under the laws of any state.

### Article IV

1. Notwithstanding any provision of this agreement to the contrary, the distribution of the Grantor's interest in the trust account shall be made in accordance with the following requirements and shall otherwise comply with section 408(a)(6) and Proposed Regulations section 1.408-8, including the incidental death benefit provisions of Proposed Regulations section 1.401(a)(9)-2, the provisions of which are herein incorporated by reference.

2. Unless otherwise elected by the time distributions are required to begin to the Grantor under paragraph 3, or to the surviving spouse under paragraph 4, other than in the case of a life annuity, life expectancies shall be recalculated annually. Such election shall be irrevocable as to the Grantor and the surviving spouse and shall apply to all subsequent years. The life expectancy of a nonspouse beneficiary may not be recalculated.

3. The Grantor's entire interest in the trust account must be, or begin to be, distributed by the Grantor's required beginning date, April 1 following the calendar year end in which the Grantor reaches age 70 1/2. By that date, the Grantor may elect, in a manner acceptable to the trustee, to have the balance in the trust account distributed in:

(a) A single sum payment.

(b) An annuity contract that provides equal or substantially equal monthly, quarterly, or annual payments over the life of the Grantor.

(c) An annuity contract that provides equal or substantially equal monthly, quarterly, or annual payments over the joint and last survivor lives of the Grantor and his or her designated beneficiary.

(d) Equal or substantially equal annual payments over a specified period that may not be longer than the Grantor's life expectancy.

(e) Equal or substantially equal annual payments over a specified period that may not be longer than the joint life and last survivor expectancy of the Grantor and his or her designated beneficiary.

4. If the Grantor dies before his or her entire interest is distributed to him or her, the entire remaining interest will be distributed as follows:

(a) If the Grantor dies on or after distribution of his or her interest has begun, distribution must continue to be made in accordance with paragraph 3.

(b) If the Grantor dies before distribution of his or her interest has begun, the entire remaining interest will, at the election of the Grantor or, if the Grantor has not so elected, at the election of the beneficiary or beneficiaries, either

(i) Be distributed by the December 31 of the year containing the fifth anniversary of the Grantor's death, or

(ii) Be distributed in equal or substantially equal payments over the life or life expectancy of the designated beneficiary or beneficiaries starting by December 31 of the year following the year of the Grantor's death. If, however, the beneficiary is the Grantor's surviving spouse, then this distribution is not required to begin before December 31 of the year in which the Grantor would have turned age 70 1/2.

(c) Except where distribution in the form of an annuity meeting the requirements of section 408(b)(3) and its related regulations has irrevocably commenced, distributions are treated as having begun on the Grantor's required beginning date, even though payments may actually have been made before that date.

(d) If the Grantor dies before his or her entire interest has been distributed and if the beneficiary is other than the surviving spouse, no additional cash contributions or rollover contributions may be accepted in the account.

Cat. No. 11810K

Form **5305** (Rev. 10-92)

---

Form 5305 (Rev. 10-92)

Page 2

5. In the case of a distribution over life expectancy in equal or substantially equal annual payments, to determine the minimum annual payment for each year, divide the Grantor's entire interest in the trust as of the close of business on December 31 of the preceding year by the life expectancy of the Grantor (or the joint life and last survivor expectancy of the Grantor and the Grantor's designated beneficiary, or the life expectancy of the designated beneficiary, whichever applies). In the case of distributions under paragraph 3, determine the initial life expectancy (or joint life and last survivor expectancy) using the attained ages of the Grantor and designated beneficiary as of their birthdays in the year the Grantor reaches age 70 1/2. In the case of a distribution in accordance with paragraph 4(b)(ii), determine life expectancy using the attained age of the designated beneficiary as of the beneficiary's birthday in the year distributions are required to commence.

6. The owner of two or more individual retirement accounts may use the "alternative method" described in Notice 88-38, 1988-1 C.B. 524, to satisfy the minimum distribution requirements described above. This method permits an individual to satisfy these requirements by taking from one individual retirement account the amount required to satisfy the requirement for another.

### Article V

1. The Grantor agrees to provide the Trustee with information necessary for the Trustee to prepare any reports required under section 408(i) and Regulations section 1.408-5 and 1.408-6.

2. The Trustee agrees to submit reports to the Internal Revenue Service and the Grantor as prescribed by the Internal Revenue Service.

### Article VI

Notwithstanding any other articles which may be added or incorporated, the provisions of Articles I through III and this sentence will be controlling. Any additional articles that are not consistent with section 408(a) and related regulations will be invalid.

### Article VII

This agreement will be amended from time to time to comply with the provisions of the Code and related regulations. Other amendments may be made with the consent of the persons whose signatures appear below.

Note: The following space (Article VIII) may be used for any other provisions you want to add. If you do not want to add any other provisions, draw a line through this space. If you do add provisions, they must comply with applicable requirements of state law and the Internal Revenue Code.

### Article VIII

Grantor's signature _____ Date _____

Trustee's signature _____ Date _____

Witness _____
(Use only if signature of the Grantor or the Trustee is required to be witnessed.)

# 6

# Distributions

A s we have seen, the purpose of an IRA or SEP-IRA is to provide the owner with retirement income. Through *distributions,* an individual withdraws money from his or her IRA or SEP.

As can be expected, there are many Internal Revenue Service rules that affect distributions. In this chapter, we'll examine when a person is required to begin taking distributions, as well as the income tax consequences of those distributions.

An IRA owner's retirement distribution may be one of the largest sums of money he or she will ever receive. Therefore, the financial representative has to be prepared to discuss the most common distribution options available with his or her clients. (Keep in mind throughout this chapter that the term "IRA" refers to "SEP" as well. The distribution rules are the same for both.)

■ ■ ■ ■ ■

## ■ GENERAL RULES FOR DISTRIBUTIONS

Although IRAs provide great investment opportunities, they are creations of federal laws and the IRS. If rules are broken regarding distributions from IRAs, penalties, some with serious financial consequences, may follow. In extreme cases, an IRA will be disqualified. Thus, a substantial distribution could be subject to immediate taxation and unforeseen penalties.

In return for years of income-tax deferral, the IRS also has definite ideas as to *when* an owner must begin receiving distributions from IRAs. The IRS considers IRAs to be tax deferred rather than tax exempt. Sooner or later, the IRS wants to collect the tax associated with IRA accumulations.

If a person receives distributions from an IRA, he or she must include them in his or her gross income for the year in which the distributions are received. A properly handled rollover (discussed in Chapter 4) is the exception to this rule.

Generally, an IRA owner may not withdraw assets, including money or other property, from an IRA without having to pay a 10 percent penalty tax (in other words, a 10 percent tax on the taxable distribution) *in addition* to the regular income tax until he or she has reached the age of 59½.

If an IRA owner receives a distribution from an IRA that includes a return of nondeductible contributions, the penalty tax does not apply to the portion of the distribution that is considered to be nontaxable.

## The Annuity Exception

If IRA owners are willing to receive distributions from their IRAs very slowly, they might be able to avoid the 10 percent penalty tax, even if those distributions begin before the IRA owner becomes age 59½.

A participant can receive distributions from an IRA that are part of a series of substantially equal payments over his or her life (or life expectancy), or over the lives (or life expectancies) of both the IRA owner and his or her beneficiary. An IRS-approved distribution method must be used and the IRA owner must make at least one distribution per year for this exception to apply. The IRS-approved distribution method will not determine a minimum distribution; rather, it will be used to calculate the *exact* amount required to be distributed each period.

The payments under this annuity exception must continue for either five years or until the IRA owner reaches age 59½, whichever is longer. This *five-year rule* does not apply if a change from an IRS-approved distribution method is a result of the death or disability of the IRA owner.

If the payments under this exception are changed for any reason other than death or disability of the IRA owner, the 10 percent penalty tax will be imposed.

## Disability/Death Exceptions

If IRA owners become disabled before reaching age 59½, they may withdraw amounts from their IRAs without having to pay the 10 percent additional tax.

The IRS will consider a taxpayer to be disabled for IRA distribution purposes if he or she cannot do "any substantial gainful activity" because of a physical or mental condition. A physician must certify that the condition has lasted, or can be expected to last, continuously for 12 months or more or that the condition can be expected to result in death. (This definition of disability mirrors the one used to determine eligibility for Social Security disability benefits.)

If an IRA owner dies before becoming age 59½, the assets in his or her IRA may be distributed to a named beneficiary or to the IRA owner's estate without being subject to the 10 percent additional tax. However, if a surviving spouse inherits an IRA from a deceased spouse and elects to treat it as his or her own, then the surviving spouse will face the 10 percent penalty for any distribution he or she might subsequently take before reaching age 59½.

### The Timely Contribution Withdrawal

If an IRA owner makes a contribution to an IRA for a given year, doesn't take a deduction for it and then withdraws the contribution before the due date (including extensions) of his or her income tax return for that year, the IRS will *not* consider the withdrawal of the contribution to be a "taxable distribution."

However, any interest or other income earned on the contribution—which also must be withdrawn—is treated as reportable income in the year in which the contribution was made. This withdrawn interest or other income may be subject to the 10 percent additional tax on early withdrawals.

## ■ REQUIRED DISTRIBUTIONS

IRA owners cannot keep funds in their IRAs indefinitely. Eventually, IRA funds must be withdrawn. The requirements for withdrawing IRA funds vary, depending on whether the party making the withdrawal is the actual IRA owner or the beneficiary of a decedent's IRA.

An IRA owner must choose to withdraw the balance in his or her IRA in one of two ways:

- by starting to withdraw *periodic distributions* of the balance in the IRA by the required beginning date or

- by withdrawing the *entire balance* in the IRA by the required beginning date.

### Age 70½ Rule

The IRS has established a definite date for beginning distribution from an IRA account balance unless the distribution has been completed or is already underway. This requirement is known as the "required beginning date" (RBD) or the "age 70½ rule."

According to this rule, if IRA distributions did not start earlier, they must start on or before April 1 of the year following the calendar year when an IRA owner becomes age 70½.

Although this first distribution isn't required to be made until April 1 of the year *after* the year in which the IRA owner reaches age 70½, the distribution actually counts *for* the year in which the owner indeed becomes 70½.

The initial required distribution is the only one that may be delayed in this way. The required minimum distribution for any year *after* the IRA owner's 70½ year must be made no later than December 31 of that later year.

Therefore, the IRA owner should receive the first distribution in the tax year when he or she truly attains age 70½ to eliminate income tax liability on *both* the first and second required distributions in a single tax year.

Sounds complicated?

Then consider this example: Bob Martin, who has not yet made any distributions from his IRA, turns 70½ in 1996. His *initial* required distribution applies to 1996—although he does not have to actually make the distribution until April 1, 1997. The *second* required distribution is applicable to 1997 and must be distributed no later than December 31, 1997. If Bob receives the first distribution in early 1997, he will need to report and owe tax on the first two required distributions in 1997.

## ■ IRA MINIMUM DISTRIBUTION REQUIREMENTS

Because the investment appreciation and some contributions to an IRA have not previously been taxed, the IRS' *minimum distribution requirements* prevent IRA owners from distributing the account balance(s) over a long period of time. In short, the minimum distribution requirements were established to limit the maximum period over which IRA distributions may be spread.

To comply with this requirement, minimum distributions from IRAs must begin no later than the "required beginning date" and must be based on one or a combination of the following payout schedules:

- the life of the owner;

- the lives of the owner and the beneficiary;

- a period certain not extending beyond the life expectancy of the owner; or

- a period certain not extending beyond the joint life expectancy of the owner and the beneficiary.

If an IRA owner has more than one beneficiary and all are individuals (rather than charities or foundations), the beneficiary with the *shortest* life expectancy will be the designated beneficiary used to determine the period over which withdrawals must be made. (According to the IRS, a *designated beneficiary* means any individual named by the IRA owner to receive his or her IRA balance upon the owner's death.)

As of the "required beginning date," IRA balances are required to make minimum distributions each year based on the life expectancy of the owner or joint life expectancy of the owner and beneficiary, if applicable. If a particular lifetime distribution option is chosen under which payments start before the required beginning date, perhaps at age 65, those payments do not fall under the minimum distribution rules, but payments after RBD must meet the rules.

Failure to satisfy the minimum distribution requirements can result in a nondeductible *50 percent penalty tax* on the difference between the amount that should have been distributed and the amount that was actually distributed.

Thus, if the minimum distribution requirement for a given year was $5,000, but the actual distribution is only $3,000, the $2,000 shortfall will be subject to the 50 percent penalty tax. This is in addition to the income tax payable on the full minimum distribution. The penalty tax is calculated as follows:

$5,000 required minimum distribution
−3,000 amount actually distributed
$2,000 excess accumulation
× .50 penalty tax
$1,000 penalty owing

## Penalty Waiver

The IRS is anxious to assure that minimum distributions are taken in a timely manner. However, the IRS doesn't want to penalize IRA owners who fail to take minimum distributions due to a "reasonable error." The IRS considers that a reasonable error may have occurred if the IRA owner:

- took incorrect advice from a plan administrator or consultant;

- incorrectly calculated the minimum distribution himself or herself; or

- misunderstood how the proper amount was to be calculated.

In cases of reasonable error, the IRS may waive the penalty after the IRA owner completes several steps. The IRA owner must first pay the penalty and then request a waiver. The waiver request is attached to his or her income tax form. If the waiver is granted, the IRS will refund the penalty paid.

## Owner Dies after Required Distributions Start

If periodic distributions that satisfy the IRS's minimum requirements have started and the IRA owner dies, any undistributed amounts at the owner's death must be paid out at least as rapidly as under the distribution method being used at the owner's death.

There is one exception to this rule: If the beneficiary is the owner's surviving spouse who elects to treat the IRA as his or her own, then the surviving spouse is considered to be the "new" owner. He or she is then subject to the same rules for required minimum distributions that normally apply to IRA owners.

## Owner Dies before Required Distributions Start

If the IRA owner dies before his or her RBD and before any distributions that satisfy the minimum distribution requirement have begun, the *entire interest* in the IRA must be distributed under one of the following choices:

- *Choice 1.* By December 31 of the *fifth* year following the owner's death.

- *Choice 2.* Over the life of the designated beneficiary or over a period not extending beyond the life expectancy of the designated beneficiary. Distributions must begin by December 31 of the year following the year of the owner's death.

In most cases, the IRA owner (or beneficiary) may predetermine (and build into the IRA documents) which choice applies. If the beneficiary makes the decision, then the decision must be made no later than December 31 of the year following the year the IRA owner died.

If no distribution decision is made, distributions must be made over the life or life expectancy of the designated beneficiary (Choice 2) if the beneficiary is the surviving spouse (which is often the case). This assumes that the spouse did not elect to treat the IRA as his or her own. If the beneficiary is *not* the surviving spouse, the IRA must be distributed by December 31 of the fifth year following the year of the owner's death (Choice 1).

As the beneficiary of a deceased spouse's IRA, the surviving spouse may decide not to treat the IRA as his or her own and instead elect an extended distribution (under Choice 2). In this case, distribution must begin no later than December 31 of the year the IRA owner (now deceased) would have reached 70½.

## Calculating Minimum Distributions

The owner of an IRA is required to figure the minimum amount that must be distributed from his or her IRA each year. Special rules apply if the IRA is an individual retirement annuity.

The required minimum distribution from an IRA can be determined by dividing the total of all IRA account values as of December 31 of the preceding year by the applicable life expectancy provided on tables supplied by the IRS.

The *applicable life expectancy* is:

- the IRA owner's remaining (single) life expectancy;

- the remaining joint life expectancy of the IRA owner and his or her designated beneficiary; or

- the remaining life expectancy of the designated beneficiary (if the IRA owner dies before distributions have begun).

Unless the IRA owner refigures his (or his spouse's) life expectancy each year, the life expectancy must be reduced by one for each year that has elapsed since the date life expectancy was first determined.

### Determining Life Expectancy

*Life expectancies,* for the purposes of the IRS, are determined from life expectancy tables, such as Table I, shown in Ill. 6.1, and Table II, shown in Ill. 6.2. To determine one's annual minimum distribution, a person must use the correct table. Table I is appropriate if the periodic payments are for the IRA owner's life only. Table II should be used if payments are for the lives of both the IRA owner and his or her beneficiary.

For distributions that start by the required beginning date, life expectancies should be determined using the ages of the owner and the beneficiary as of their birthdays in the IRA owner's 70½ year. If the owner dies before distributions have begun, the designated beneficiary's life expectancy is determined from Table I using the beneficiary's age based on his or her birthday in the year that distributions must begin.

| ILL. 6.1 ■ Table I — IRS Life Expectancy Table for Single Life | | | |
|---|---|---|---|
| Age | Life Expectancy | Age | Life Expectancy |
| 56 | 27.7 | 71 | 15.3 |
| 57 | 26.8 | 72 | 14.6 |
| 58 | 25.9 | 73 | 13.9 |
| 59 | 25.0 | 74 | 13.2 |
| 60 | 24.2 | 75 | 12.5 |
| 61 | 23.3 | 76 | 11.9 |
| 62 | 22.5 | 77 | 11.2 |
| 63 | 21.6 | 78 | 10.6 |
| 64 | 20.8 | 79 | 10.0 |
| 65 | 20.0 | 80 | 9.5 |
| 66 | 19.2 | 81 | 8.9 |
| 67 | 18.4 | 82 | 8.4 |
| 68 | 17.6 | 83 | 7.9 |
| 69 | 16.8 | 84 | 7.4 |
| 70 | 16.0 | 85 | 6.9 |

(Complete Table I can be found in Appendix E of IRS Publication 590.)

Let's say that 70-year-old Ed has an IRA and must take a minimum distribution. The value of the IRA as of December 31 last year was $250,000. If he chose to take distributions over his single life expectancy, the amount due for this year would be $15,625 ($250,000 divided by 16.0). If he chose to take distributions over the joint-life expectancy of himself and his 66-year-old wife, Clara, the minimum due this year would be $11,111 ($250,000 divided by 22.5).

### Refiguring Life Expectancy

Most IRA plan documents require that the life of the IRA owner (and his or her spouse, if the spouse is designated as joint beneficiary) must be *refigured* each year when calculating the required minimum distribution due. *Refiguring life expectancy* simply means returning to the appropriate IRS life expectancy table—single or joint life, whichever was elected for RMD purposes—and using the owner's (and spouse's, if applicable) *actual* age according to his or her birthday (and the spouse's birthday) during the specific tax year to determine the applicable life expectancy divisor.

For example, let's return to Ed and Clara and assume Ed elected a joint-life payout period for his required distributions. For the first distribution, when Ed is 71 and Clara is 66, the joint period is 22.2 years (see Ill. 6.2). If they were to refigure life expectancy, they would return to Table II in the second year determine a new joint life period based on their attained ages—Ed is now 72 and Clara is 67. A refigured joint life expectancy for year two is 21.3 years. This would be the divisor used to calculate the RMD for the second year. The third year it would be 20.5, the fourth year it would be 19.6, and so on.

## ILL. 6.2 ■ Table II — IRS Life Expectancy Table for Joint Lives

| Participant's Age | Beneficiary's Age | | | | | | | | | | | | | |
| --- | --- | --- | --- | --- | --- | --- | --- | --- | --- | --- | --- | --- | --- | --- |
| | 55 | 56 | 57 | 58 | 59 | 60 | 61 | 62 | 63 | 64 | 65 | 66 | 67 | 68 |
| 70 | 29.9 | 29.1 | 28.4 | 27.6 | 26.9 | 26.2 | 25.6 | 24.9 | 24.3 | 23.7 | 23.1 | 22.5 | 22.0 | 21.5 |
| 71 | 29.7 | 29.0 | 28.2 | 27.5 | 26.7 | 26.0 | 25.3 | 24.7 | 24.0 | 23.4 | 22.8 | 22.2 | 21.7 | 21.2 |
| 72 | 29.6 | 28.8 | 28.1 | 27.3 | 26.5 | 25.8 | 25.1 | 24.4 | 23.8 | 23.1 | 22.5 | 21.9 | 21.3 | 20.8 |
| 73 | 29.5 | 28.7 | 27.9 | 27.1 | 26.4 | 25.6 | 24.9 | 24.2 | 23.5 | 22.9 | 22.2 | 21.6 | 21.0 | 20.5 |
| 74 | 29.4 | 28.6 | 27.8 | 27.0 | 26.2 | 25.5 | 24.7 | 24.0 | 23.3 | 22.7 | 22.0 | 21.4 | 20.8 | 20.2 |
| 75 | 29.3 | 28.5 | 27.7 | 26.9 | 26.1 | 25.3 | 24.6 | 23.8 | 23.1 | 22.4 | 21.8 | 21.1 | 20.5 | 19.9 |

(Complete Table II can be found in Appendix E of IRS Publication 490.)

On the other hand, the terms of some IRAs may allow the owner to elect not to refigure life expectancy. In these cases, the IRA owner simply subtracts one (1) from the first and subsequent life expectancy periods. Continuing with our example, if Ed elected not to refigure the couple's joint life expectancy, the divisor for year two would be 21.2, for year three it would be 20.2, for year four it would be 19.2 and so on.

There are a number of important points to note about refiguring life expectancy:

1. The election to refigure or not refigure must be made by the date the first required minimum distribution is due.

2. If a joint life expectancy is refigured annually and either the IRA owner or the spouse dies, then the survivor's life is used to calculate minimum distributions for the years after the death occurred.

3. If life expectancies are refigured each year and the IRA owner dies and then the spouse dies after the required distribution date, the entire value of the IRA must be distributed before the last day of the year after the surviving spouse's death.

4. Although the life of the IRA owner may always be refigured, for beneficiaries, only spouses' lives may be refigured. If the IRA beneficiary is not the spouse and a joint life election is made and the owner elects to refigure his or her own life, then an additional calculation must be performed to determine the appropriate RMD for any given year. This calculation is the same as that used for the minimum distribution incidental benefit requirement, which is explained on the following page.

### Minimum Distribution Incidental Benefit Requirement

Distributions from an IRA during the owner's lifetime must meet the *minimum distribution incidental benefit*, or MDIB, requirement. The MDIB basically says that when calculating the joint-life expectancy of an IRA owner and a nonspouse beneficiary, the difference in ages cannot exceed 10 years. The IRS imposes this requirement to ensure that IRAs are used mainly to provide retirement benefits for

## ILL. 6.3 ■ Table for Determining Applicable Divisor for MDIB (Minimum Distribution Incidental Benefit)

| Age | Applicable divisor | Age | Applicable divisor |
|-----|--------------------|-----|--------------------|
| 70 | 26.2 | 93 | 8.8 |
| 71 | 25.3 | 94 | 8.3 |
| 72 | 24.4 | 95 | 7.8 |
| 73 | 23.5 | 96 | 7.3 |
| 74 | 22.7 | 97 | 6.9 |
| 75 | 21.8 | 98 | 6.5 |
| 76 | 20.9 | 99 | 6.1 |
| 77 | 20.1 | 100 | 5.7 |
| 78 | 19.2 | 101 | 5.3 |
| 79 | 18.4 | 102 | 5.0 |
| 80 | 17.6 | 103 | 4.7 |
| 81 | 16.8 | 104 | 4.4 |
| 82 | 16.0 | 105 | 4.1 |
| 83 | 15.3 | 106 | 3.8 |
| 84 | 14.5 | 107 | 3.6 |
| 85 | 13.8 | 108 | 3.3 |
| 86 | 13.1 | 109 | 3.1 |
| 87 | 12.4 | 110 | 2.8 |
| 88 | 11.8 | 111 | 2.6 |
| 89 | 11.1 | 112 | 2.4 |
| 90 | 10.5 | 113 | 2.2 |
| 91 | 9.9 | 114 | 2.0 |
| 92 | 9.4 | 115+ | 1.8 |

their owners. After the IRA owner's death, only "incidental" benefits are expected to stay in the IRA to be paid out to the beneficiary. Essentially, this requirement lessens the advantage to naming a very young person as a joint-life beneficiary of one's IRA.

To calculate a required minimum distribution that also satisfies the MDIB rules, the IRA owner must complete the following steps. As you can see, these steps are for the RMD in year one and for the RMD in subsequent years.

### MDIB Requirement for Year One RMD

*Step 1*: Using the "Table for Determining Applicable Divisor for MDIB," (Ill. 6.3), find the applicable divisor for the IRA owner's age. The IRA owner should use the age that corresponds to his or her birthday in the year for which the distribution is being figured.

*Step 2*: The IRA owner compares the MDIB divisor against the joint-life expectancy period from Table II. The *smaller* of these two is used to calculate the RMD in the first year. (Note: In cases where the nonspouse beneficiary is more than 10 years younger than the IRA owner, the MDIB divisor will always be smaller and thus, will always be the one used.)

*Step 3*: The RMD for year one is calculated by dividing the total amount in the owner's IRAs as of December 31 of the preceding year by the (smaller) number in Step 2.

For example, let's say Oliver, born October 1, 1925, became 70½ in 1996. The value of his sole IRA as of December 31, 1995, was $58,000. Oliver's IRA beneficiary is his 56-year old brother, Sam. Oliver knows that he has to take a minimum distribution from his IRA for 1996. He elects to have his required distributions based on the joint-life expectancy of himself and his brother. He also elects to refigure his own life expectancy; his brother's cannot be refigured. For the RMD for 1996, Oliver must use the divisor in the MDIB table, since his beneficiary is more than 10 years younger than he is. Thus, Oliver's required distribution for 1996 is $2,292 ($58,000 divided by 25.3). Assuming no other withdrawals, his adjusted 1996 account balance, which will be used for calculating his 1997 distribution, is $55,708. (For purposes of this example, interest earnings on the declining IRA balance have been ignored.)

### MDIB Requirement for Year Two (and Beyond) RMD

Now let's move ahead. It's one year later and time again for Oliver to take the required distribution from his IRA. That will be his adjusted IRA balance as of December 31, 1996, or $55,708, divided by his and Sam's joint life expectancy. Remember, Oliver elected to refigure his own life, but cannot refigure his brother's life. The joint life expectancy for year two is calculated as follows:

*Step 1*: Life expectancy of the beneficiary, using his age as of his birthday in the first distribution year (i.e., in 1996), based on single life expectancy table (Table I) . . . . . . . . . . . . . . . . . . . . . . . . . . . . . . . . . 27.7

*Step 2*: Number of years that have passed since first distribution year . . . . . . . . 1.0

*Step 3*: Remaining life expectancy of beneficiary (Step 1 minus Step 2) . . . . . . 26.7

*Step 4*: Divisor in Table I that is closest to but less than the amount in Step 3. Enter the age shown for that divisor amount . . . . . . . . . . . . . . . 58

*Step 5*: IRA owner's age as of his or her birthday this year . . . . . . . . . . . . . . . . 72

*Step 6*: Joint life expectancy of ages in Step 4 and Step 5, using Table II . . . . . 27.3

*Step 7*: Applicable divisor from MDIB table, based on owner's age in Step 5 . . . . . . . . . . . . . . . . . . . . . . . . . . . . . . . . . . . . . . . . . . . . . . . 24.4

*Step 8*: Refigured life expectancy (using *smaller* of Step 6 and Step 7) . . . . . . . 24.4

Oliver's required minimum distribution for 1997, using the refigured life expectancy, is $2,283 ($55,708 divided by 24.4).

The MDIB requirement doesn't apply to distributions paid in years after the death of an original IRA account owner. Consequently, if an individual holds an IRA as a beneficiary of a deceased IRA owner, minimum distributions from the IRA can be calculated using the general rules for distributions.

### Miscellaneous Rules for Minimum Distributions

The yearly minimum distribution can be taken however the owner desires (all at once or periodically, such as monthly or quarterly) as long as the total distributions for the year equal the required minimum amount. Remember, an IRA owner can always take *more* than the required minimum.

If an individual has more than one IRA, he or she must determine the minimum distribution separately for each IRA. However, the owner may total the minimum amounts from all IRAs and take the total from any one or more of the IRA accounts.

For example, Harry Penworthy is 72 and his wife is 66. He has two IRAs. Harry's account balance in IRA A is $10,000; his account balance in IRA B is $20,000. Harry elects a single life payout for IRA A ($10,000 divided by 14.6, the single life expectancy as shown in Ill. 6.1) and a joint life payout for IRA B ($20,000 divided by 21.9, the joint life expectancy of Harry and his wife as shown in Ill. 6.2). The total required distribution that must be taken from Harry's IRAs is $1,598 ($685 plus $913). Harry can take $1,598 from IRA A or IRA B, or he can take distributions from both IRAs as long as they total $1,598.

If an individual takes more in any year than the required minimum amount for that year, he or she will not receive credit for the additional amount when figuring the minimum distribution amounts for future years. The exception to this involves required distributions in the 70½ year. Any amount distributed in the 70½ year will be credited toward the amount that must be distributed no later than April 1 of the following year.

## ■ TAX TREATMENT OF DISTRIBUTIONS

IRA owners must report IRA distributions in their gross incomes in the year when the distributions are received. Exceptions to this general rule include rollovers, timely withdrawals of contributions and the return of nondeductible contributions.

IRA distributions are taxed as ordinary income. Special averaging (e.g., five-year or ten-year forward averaging) for lump-sum distributions is not available with IRA distributions. Also, IRA distributions are not treated as capital gains.

### Fully or Partially Taxable Distributions?

An individual's IRA distribution may be fully or partially taxable, depending on whether his or her IRA includes only deductible contributions or any nondeductible contributions.

If only deductible contributions were made to a person's IRA (or IRAs, if he or she has more than one) at any time, then he or she has no "basis" in the IRA. Because the person has no basis in the IRA, any distributions are fully taxable in the year when they are received.

If a IRA owner made nondeductible contributions to any of his or her IRAs, figuring tax liability becomes more complicated. The IRA owner has a cost basis (after-tax investment in the IRA) to the extent of the nondeductible contributions. Such nondeductible contributions are *not* taxed when they are distributed from the IRA. They are considered to be a return of the owner's after-tax invested capital.

### ILL 6.4 ■ Figuring Taxable and Nontaxable Portions of an IRA Distribution

Over the years, Karen made the following contributions to her IRAs:

| Year | Deductible Contribution | Nondeductible Contribution |
|------|------------------------|---------------------------|
| 1986 | $2,000 | -0- |
| 1987 | 2,000 | -0- |
| 1988 | 2,000 | -0- |
| 1989 | 1,000 | -0- |
| 1990 | 1,000 | -0- |
| 1991 | 700 | $300 |
| 1992 | 700 | 300 |
| Total contributions | $9,400 | $600 |

Though she stopped making contributions to her accounts years ago, thanks to interest earnings, Karen's IRAs have grown. As of December 31 last year, her funds were valued at $20,000. Last year, she also took her first distribution which was $5,000. If Karen did not have any basis in her IRAs, the full $5,000 would be taxable. However, given that she has a $600 cost basis in her plans, a portion of that $5,000 distribution will be received tax free. Here is how Karen would calculate the taxable and nontaxable portions of this distribution:

| | |
|---|---|
| Value of IRA(s) as of December 31, last year plus any distribution taken last year: | $25,000 |
| Karen's total IRA cost basis: | 600 |
| Cost basis as a percent of total IRA value ($600 ÷ $25,000): | .024 |
| Nontaxable portion of the distribution: ($5,000 × .024) | $ 120 |
| Taxable portion of the distribution: ($5,000 − $120) | $ 4,880 |

Karen's cost basis in her IRAs is now reduced by $120 to $480. She would continue to follow the above steps, adjusting the percentage of cost basis for each year a distribution is taken, until she recovers her full $600 cost basis. From that point on, all distributions would be fully taxable.

Note in this example that the IRA owner stopped making contributions to her plan before she began taking any distributions. In cases where a contribution, whether deductible or nondeductible, is made for a year in which a distribution is taken, a different approach to determine the distribution's taxable and nontaxable portions is necessary. This is explained on page 69.

When IRA distributions are paid, special rules must be followed to compute the tax on the distributions if:

- only nondeductible contributions were made and there have been earnings or gains or

- if both deductible and nondeductible contributions were made.

Only the part of the distribution that represents the IRA owner's cost basis (the nondeductible contributions) is tax free. For IRAs that contain nondeductible contributions, distributions will be considered to consist partly of nondeductible contributions (basis) and partly of deductible contributions, earnings or gains. Thus, until a taxpayer fully recovers his or her basis in the IRA, each distribution is partly taxable and partly nontaxable. (Illustration 6.4 contains an example that explains the concept of figuring the taxable and nontaxable portions of a distribution. In practice, however, IRA owners should use Form 8606.)

### *Form 8606*

An individual is required to complete Form 8606 (shown at the end of this chapter) if he or she received an IRA distribution and, at any time, made nondeductible IRA contributions. The individual may use the form to figure the nontaxable distributions for a given tax year and the total IRA basis for the current and earlier years. The individual is required to attach Form 8606 to his or her regular income tax Form 1040.

### Contributions and Distributions in the Same Year

In many cases, it's not unusual for an IRA owner to take a distribution in the same year he or she makes a contribution. If an IRA owner makes an IRA contribution that may be nondeductible because he or she is covered by an employer retirement plan, the IRA owner also needs to use a special worksheet. The worksheet helps the IRA owner determine the amount that must be included in income for any part of the IRA distribution that represents deductible contributions, earnings or gains. If the IRA owner has more than one IRA, he or she must consider the distributions together as if they were a single IRA.

If an IRA owner is, in fact, covered by an employer plan and has made IRA contributions for the current year that may be deductible, the following worksheet can be used to determine how much of his or her current year IRA distribution is tax free and how much is taxable.

1. Enter the basis in all IRA(s) as of December 31, last year.     $_____

2. Enter all IRA contributions made for this year, regardless of whether they are deductible (contributions to be made from January 1 through April 15 of next year should be included; however, do not include contributions rolled over from retirement plans).     $_____

3. Add Steps 1 and 2.     $_____

4. Enter the value of all IRA(s) as of December 31 this year (include any outstanding rollovers).     $_____

5. Enter the total IRA distributions received this year (do not include outstanding rollovers).     $_____

6. Add Steps 4 and 5.     $_____

7. Divide Step 3 by Step 6. Enter the result as a decimal (to at least two places), but do not enter more than 1.00.     _____

8. Nontaxable portion of the distribution (multiply Step 5 by Step 7).     $_____

9. Taxable portion of the distribution (subtract Step 8 from Step 5).     $_____

### Recognizing Losses on IRA Investments

If an IRA owner has a loss on his or her IRA investment, then he or she can recognize the loss on his or her income-tax return, but only when all the amounts in all of his or her IRA accounts have been distributed and the total distributions are less than his or her unrecovered basis—the total amount of the nondeductible contributions in the IRA. He or she can claim the loss as a miscellaneous itemized deduction as long as the total of miscellaneous itemized deductions exceeds 2 percent of adjusted gross income.

For example, Brian has made nondeductible contributions to an IRA totaling $2,000, giving him a basis of $2,000 at the end of 1994. By the end of 1995, his IRA earned $400 of interest income. In that year, Brian withdrew $600, reducing the value of his IRA to $1,800 at year's end. Using Form 8606 to help him with his calculations, Brian determines the taxable part of the distribution and his remaining basis.

In 1996, Brian's IRA had a *loss* of $500. At the end of that year, Brian's IRA balance was $1,300. Brian's remaining basis in his IRA is $1,500. Brian withdrew the $1,300 balance remaining in the IRA. He can claim a loss for 1996 of $200 (the $1,300 withdrawn less the remaining $1,500 cost basis).

### Inherited IRAs

The beneficiaries of participants' IRAs must include distributions to them in their gross incomes. Beneficiaries can be virtually anyone the IRA owner chooses to receive the benefits of his or her IRA. A spousal beneficiary can elect to treat the entire inherited interest as his or her own IRA.

A nonspousal beneficiary may not treat an inherited IRA as though the beneficiary established it. The IRA can neither be rolled into nor receive a rollover from another IRA. No deduction will be permitted for amounts deposited into an inherited IRA. Also, nondeductible contributions cannot be made into an IRA that is inherited by a nonspousal beneficiary.

If an individual inherits an IRA from a deceased owner who had a basis in the IRA due to nondeductible contributions, then that basis remains with the IRA and it carries over to the beneficiary.

However, beneficiaries may not claim a death benefit exclusion (as is available with certain distributions from qualified plans) for any part of the distribution from an inherited IRA.

### IRAs and the Federal Estate Tax

Beneficiaries of participants' IRAs may be able to claim a federal estate tax deduction for certain distributions from a decedent's IRA. If a beneficiary receives a lump-sum distribution from an IRA, the IRS taxes it as "income in respect to the decedent" to the extent of net IRA balance. (This refers to the balance as of the date of death minus the IRA owner's basis.)

## ILL. 6.5 ■ Part of Form 1040 (Line 16b)

| | | | | |
|---|---|---|---|---|
| **Income** | 7 | Wages, salaries, tips, etc. Attach Form(s) W-2 . . . . . . . . . . . . . . . . . . . . . . . . . . . . . . . . . . . | 7 | |
| | 8a | Taxable interest income (see page 15). Attach Schedule B if over $400 . . . . . . . . . . . . . . . . | 8a | |
| **Attach** | b | Tax-exempt interest (see page 16). DON'T include on line 8a ☐ 8b ☐ | | |
| **Copy B of your** | 9 | Dividend income. Attach Schedule B if over $400 . . . . . . . . . . . . . . . . . . . . . . . . . . . . . . . . | 9 | |
| **Forms W-2,** **W-2G, and** | 10 | Taxable refunds, credits, or offsets of state and local income taxes (see page 16) . . . . . . . . . | 10 | |
| **1099-R here.** | 11 | Alimony received . . . . . . . . . . . . . . . . . . . . . . . . . . . . . . . . . . . . . . . . . . . . . . . . . . . . . . . . | 11 | |
| **If you did not** | 12 | Business income or (loss). Attach Schedule C or C-EZ . . . . . . . . . . . . . . . . . . . . . . . . . . . . | 12 | |
| **get a W-2, see** | 13 | Capital gain or (loss). If required, attach Schedule D (see page 16) . . . . . . . . . . . . . . . . . . . | 13 | |
| **page 15.** | 14 | Other gains or (losses). Attach Form 4797 . . . . . . . . . . . . . . . . . . . . . . . . . . . . . . . . . . . . . . | 14 | |
| | 15a | Total IRA distributions . . . ☐ 15a ☐ b Taxable amount (see page 17) | 15b | |
| **Enclose, but do** **not attach, any** | 16a | Total pensions and annuities ☐ 16a ☐ b Taxable amount (see page 17) | 16b | |
| **payment with** | 17 | Rental real estate, royalties, partnerships, S corporations, trusts, etc. Attach Schedule E . . . . | 17 | |
| **your return.** | 18 | Farm income or (loss). Attach Schedule F . . . . . . . . . . . . . . . . . . . . . . . . . . . . . . . . . . . . . . | 18 | |
| | 19 | Unemployment compensation (see page 18) . . . . . . . . . . . . . . . . . . . . . . . . . . . . . . . . . . . . | 19 | |
| | 20a | Social security benefits ☐ 20a ☐ b Taxable amount (see page 18) | 20b | |
| | 21 | Other income. List type and amount- see page 18 _____ | 21 | |
| | 22 | Add the amounts in the far right column for lines 7 through 21. This is your total income . . . ▶ | 22 | |

Because the IRS generally adheres to the notion that distributions should face federal taxation only once, when the beneficiary reports income in respect to a decedent, he or she can deduct the part of federal estate tax that corresponds to that income.

### Distribution in the Form of an Annuity

The IRA owner may tell his or her IRA custodian to use the amount in the account to buy an annuity contract. No tax consequences occur when the new owner acquires the annuity contract. However, the new owner will be taxed when he or she starts receiving payments from that annuity contract. If only deductible contributions were made to the IRA since it was set up, the annuity payments are fully taxable. If an owner's IRA includes both deductible and nondeductible contributions, the annuity payments will be partially taxable. Amounts corresponding to the owner's basis will be excluded from tax liability because the owner has already paid taxes on that money.

### Reporting and Withholding Requirements for Taxable Amounts

A custodian is required to withhold federal income tax from IRA distributions unless the owner chooses not to have tax withheld. When IRA owners receive a distribution from their IRAs, they will be sent Form 1099-R—"Distributions from Pensions, Annuities, Retirement or Profit-Sharing Plans, IRAs, Insurance Contracts, etc.," which is shown at the end of this chapter.

The tax withheld from an annuity or a similar payment is based on the owner's marital status and the number of exemptions claimed on a "withholding certificate" (Form W-4P). A taxpayer who does not file a certificate will be treated for withholding purposes as a married individual claiming three withholding allowances.

For the most part, custodians will withhold 10 percent on lump-sum distributions. Special rules apply for U.S citizens living outside the United States.

### Reporting Taxable Distributions

IRA owners who receive taxable distributions from their IRAs, including premature distributions, will report them on the appropriate lines of their Form 1040 or 1040As. They cannot be reported on the more simplified Form 1040EZ.

## ■ EXCESS DISTRIBUTIONS

If IRA owners receive distributions over $155,000 (indexed for inflation) in one year from all their retirement accounts, they may have to pay a 15 percent tax for excess distributions. This 15 percent tax applies to IRAs, SEP-IRAs, any qualified employer plan and tax-sheltered annuities.

However, this tax does not apply to:

- distributions after the death of the IRA owner (or employee in the case of employer plans);

- distributions that are rolled over;

- distributions that represent nondeductible contributions; and

- corrections after an individual makes excess contributions to an IRA or qualified plan.

### Excess Estate Tax

If an IRA owner decides to avoid paying the excise tax by simply letting large amounts in retirement accounts remain there until his or her death, he or she should consider this: for individuals dying after December 31, 1986, the *estate* tax will be increased by 15 percent of the "excess retirement accumulation." In short, the IRS intends to get its excise tax sooner or later.

The *excess retirement accumulation* is the aggregate value of the decedent's interest in all qualified employer plans, tax-sheltered annuities, qualified annuity plans, and IRAs that represents more than the value of a single life annuity that would generate annual payments of $155,000 (indexed) over the decedent's remaining life expectancy. Unlike the regular estate tax, no credits may be applied to reduce this tax.

## ■ SUMMARY

As time goes on and more people with IRAs and SEPs reach their retirement years, there will be growing concern about the rules and procedures for distributing the IRA money. The IRS insists that taxpayers begin withdrawals from their IRAs/SEPs by certain dates.

From age 59½, IRA owners no longer have to pay the 10 percent penalty tax for taking money out of an IRA. Between ages 59½ and 70½, IRA owners have the greatest flexibility in taking distributions from their IRAs. Within this age window, an IRA owner can pay himself or herself as much or as little as he or she likes, although most distributions will be taxable.

Inherited IRAs also have to be distributed. However, a beneficiary, who is also the spouse of the deceased owner, may choose to treat the IRA as his or her own and then wait many years before making distributions from the inherited IRA.

Distributions considered to be income from retirement accounts in excess of $155,000 annually are subject to a 15 percent excise tax, which is levied in addition to the ordinary income tax.

### ■ CHAPTER 6 QUESTIONS FOR REVIEW

1. Which of the following is *not* an exception to the 10 percent penalty that generally applies to distributions from an IRA before the owner reaches age 59½?

   a. The IRA owner becomes disabled.
   b. The IRA owner dies.
   c. The IRA owner receives an annuity-type distribution.
   d. The IRA owner becomes unemployed.

2. An IRA owner can meet the minimum distribution requirement by

   a. starting to withdraw periodic distributions of the balance in the IRA by the required beginning date.
   b. withdrawing the entire balance in the IRA by the required beginning date.
   c. Both a and b
   d. Neither a nor b

3. Who may treat an inherited IRA as his or her own?

   a. Any beneficiary
   b. The surviving spouse of the decedent
   c. Both a and b
   d. Neither a nor b

4. The "required beginning date" corresponding with an IRA is

   a. the IRA owner's 59½ birthday.
   b. the IRA owner's 70½ birthday.
   c. April 1 of the year following the year in which the IRA owner becomes 70½.
   d. April 15 of the year following the year in which the IRA owner becomes 70½.

5. If the minimum distribution requirement for a given year was $4,000, but the actual IRA distribution is only $3,000, the penalty is

   a. $2,000.
   b. $1,000.
   c. $500.
   d. $250.

6. To report nontaxable IRA distributions, a taxpayer is required to file

   a. Form 1040.
   b. Form 5500.
   c. Form 8606.
   d. Form 1099-R.

7. Ann Parker, who has two IRAs, became 70½ on February 1, 1995. She must start receiving her IRA distributions by

   a. April 1, 1995.
   b. April 15, 1995.
   c. January 1, 1996.
   d. April 1, 1996.

406 9-94

3859

**Form 8606**

Department of the Treasury
Internal Revenue Service

## Nondeductible IRAs
### (Contributions, Distributions, and Basis)
▶ Please see What Records Must I Keep? on page 2.
▶ Attach to Form 1040, Form 1040A, or Form 1040NR.

OMB No. 1545-1007

**1994**

Attachment
Sequence No. 47

Name. If married, file a separate Form 8606 for each spouse. See instructions.

Your social security number

**Fill in Your Address Only If You Are Filing This Form by Itself and Not With Your Tax Return** ▶

Home address (number and street, or P.O. box if mail is not delivered to your home)

Apt. no.

City, town or post office, state, and ZIP code

### Contributions, Nontaxable Distributions, and Basis

| | | |
|---|---|---|
| 1 | Enter your IRA contributions for 1994 that you choose to be nondeductible. Include those made during 1/1/95–4/17/95 that were for 1994. See instructions | 1 |
| 2 | Enter your total IRA basis for 1993 and earlier years. See instructions | 2 |
| 3 | Add lines 1 and 2 | 3 |

**Did you receive any IRA distributions (withdrawals) in 1994?**

No ──▶ Enter the amount from line 3 on line 12. Then, stop and read **When and Where To File** on page 2.

Yes ──▶ Go to line 4.

| | | |
|---|---|---|
| 4 | Enter only those contributions included on line 1 that were made during 1/1/95–4/17/95. This amount will be the same as line 1 if all of your nondeductible contributions for 1994 were made in 1995 by 4/17/95. See instructions | 4 |
| 5 | Subtract line 4 from line 3 | 5 |
| 6 | Enter the total value of **ALL** your IRAs as of 12/31/94 plus any outstanding rollovers. See instructions | 6 |
| 7 | Enter the total IRA distributions received during 1994. Do not include amounts rolled over before 1/1/95. See instructions | 7 |
| 8 | Add lines 6 and 7 | 8 |
| 9 | Divide line 5 by line 8 and enter the result as a decimal (to at least two places). Do not enter more than "1.00" | 9 × . |
| 10 | Multiply line 7 by line 9. This is the amount of your **nontaxable distributions for 1994** | 10 |
| 11 | Subtract line 10 from line 5. This is the **basis in your IRA(s) as of 12/31/94** | 11 |
| 12 | Add lines 4 and 11. This is your **total IRA basis for 1994 and earlier years** | 12 |

### Taxable Distributions for 1994

| | | |
|---|---|---|
| 13 | Subtract line 10 from line 7. Enter the result here and on Form 1040, line 15b; Form 1040A, line 10b; or Form 1040NR, line 16b, whichever applies | 13 |

**Sign Here Only If You Are Filing This Form by Itself and Not With Your Tax Return**

Under penalties of perjury, I declare that I have examined this form, including accompanying attachments, and to the best of my knowledge and belief, it is true, correct, and complete.

▶ Your signature

▶ Date

## Paperwork Reduction Act Notice

We ask for the information on this form to carry out the Internal Revenue laws of the United States. You are required to give us the information. We need it to ensure that you are complying with these laws and to allow us to figure and collect the right amount of tax.

The time needed to complete and file this form will vary depending on individual circumstances. The estimated average time is: **Recordkeeping**, 26 min.; **Learning about the law or the form**, 7 min.; **Preparing the form**, 21 min.; and **Copying, assembling, and sending the form to the IRS**, 20 min.

If you have comments concerning the accuracy of these time estimates or suggestions for making this form more

simple, we would be happy to hear from you. You can write to both the IRS and the Office of Management and Budget at the addresses listed in the Instructions for Form 1040, Form 1040A, or Form 1040NR.

## General Instructions

*Section references are to the Internal Revenue Code.*

### Purpose of Form

Use Form 8606 to report your IRA contributions that you choose to be nondeductible. For example, if you cannot deduct all of your contributions because of the income limits for IRAs, you may want to make nondeductible contributions.

Also use Form 8606 to figure the basis in your IRA(s) and the taxable part of any distributions you received in 1994 if you have ever made nondeductible contributions.

Your **basis** is the total of all your nondeductible IRA contributions minus the total of all nontaxable IRA distributions received. It is to your advantage to keep track of your basis because it is used to figure the nontaxable part of future distributions.

**Note:** *To figure your deductible IRA contributions, use the Instructions for Form 1040 or Form 1040A, whichever applies.*

### Who Must File

You must file Form 8606 for 1994 if:

● You made nondeductible contributions to your IRA for 1994, **or**

● You received IRA distributions in 1994 **and** you have ever made nondeductible contributions to any of your IRAs.

Cat.No. 63966F

Form **8606** (1994)

# IRS Form 1099-R

410  11-94

|CAUTION: The IRS will not accept photocopies of Copy A. See the 1995 instructions for the Form 1099 series.—CCH.|

**2215-9**

9898  ☐ VOID   ☐ CORRECTED

| PAYER'S name, street address, city, state, and ZIP code | 1 Gross distribution $ | OMB No. 1545-0119 **1995** Form **1099-R** | **Distributions From Pensions, Annuities, Retirement or Profit-Sharing Plans, IRAs, Insurance Contracts, etc.** |
|---|---|---|---|
| | 2a Taxable amount $ | | |
| | 2b Taxable amount not determined ☐ | Total distribution ☐ | **Copy A For Internal Revenue Service Center** |
| PAYER'S Federal identification number | RECIPIENT'S identification number | 3 Capital gain (included in box 2a) $ | 4 Federal income tax withheld $ | File with Form 1096. |
| RECIPIENT'S name | 5 Employee contributions or insurance premiums $ | 6 Net unrealized appreciation in employer's securities $ | For Paperwork Reduction Act Notice and instructions for completing this form, see **Instructions for Forms 1099, 1098, 5498, and W-2G.** |
| Street address (including apt. no.) | 7 Distribution code / IRA/SEP ☐ | 8 Other $ % | |
| City, state, and ZIP code | 9a Your percentage of total distribution % | 9b Total employee contributions $ | |
| Account number (optional) | 10 State tax withheld $ $ | 11 State/Payer's state no. | 12 State distribution $ $ |
| | 13 Local tax withheld $ $ | 14 Name of locality | 15 Local distribution $ $ |

Form **1099-R**    Cat. No. 14436Q    Department of the Treasury - Internal Revenue Service

**Do NOT Cut or Separate Forms on This Page**

# ..... Answer Key

**CHAPTER 1**

1. b
2. b
3. d
4. b
5. c
6. c
7. d

**CHAPTER 2**

1. c
2. c
3. a
4. b
5. c

**CHAPTER 3**

1. d
2. a
3. c
4. d
5. a
6. c

**CHAPTER 4**

1. c
2. c
3. b
4. a
5. b
6. c

**CHAPTER 5**

1. d
2. c
3. a
4. d
5. c
6. a
7. c

**CHAPTER 6**

1. d
2. c
3. b
4. c
5. c
6. c
7. d

77